TO INSPIRE COURAGE SPIRIT CHARACTER

Copyright © YFC and CWR 2012

Published 2012 by CWR, Waverley Abbey House, Waverley Lane, Farnham, Surrey GU9 8EP, England. Registered Charity No. 294387. Registered Limited Company No. 1990308.

Mettle Bible-reading notes are produced in association with British Youth for Christ. British Youth for Christ is part of Youth for Christ International, a movement of youth evangelism organisations in over 100 countries of the world. Please visit www.yfci.org for the country nearest you.

Series Editor: Simeon Whiting
Contributors: Chris Kidd, Hannah Kidd, Steve Warner and Simeon Whiting.

The notes on 'Jesus, fully man and fully God' are adapted from those previously published in *Mettle* September–December 2008.

All rights reserved. No part of this publication may be reproduced, stored in a retrieval system, or transmitted, in any form or by any means, electronic, mechanical, photocopying, recording or otherwise, without the prior permission in writing of CWR.

See back of book for list of National Distributors.

Unless otherwise indicated, all Scripture references are from the Holy Bible, New Living Translations (NLT), copyright © 1996, revised 2004. Used by permission of Tyndale House Publishers, Inc., Wheaton, Illinois 60189. All rights reserved.

Other quotations are marked:
NIV: Scripture quotations taken from The Holy Bible, New International Version (Anglicised edition) Copyright ©1979, 1984, 2011 by Biblica (formerly International Bible Society). Used by permission of Hodder & Stoughton Publishers, an Hachette UK company. All rights reserved.

Concept development by YFC and CWR.

Editing, design and production by CWR.

Printed in Wales by Stevens & George Print Group.

CONTENTS

JESUS, FULLY MAN + FULLY GOD PART 1		4
HEALTH PART 1		16
FUN PART 1		30
DISCIPLINE PART 1		44
JESUS, FULLY MAN + FULLY GOD PART 2		58
HEALTH PART 2		72
FUN PART 2		86
DISCIPLINE PART 2		100
JESUS, FULLY MAN + FULLY GOD PART 3		114

WELCOME TO mettle
COURAGE SPIRIT CHARACTER ...

WELCOME TO this new issue of *Mettle*.
In our core readings, we'll look at the life of Jesus and at why we believe He is fully man and fully God at the same time. This idea is crucial to our faith, so let's think about why we believe it!

Our 'hot potatoes' are nice and varied. We'll think about 'Health': how can we be healthy in our thoughts, attitudes and faith, as well as in our bodies? For something a little bit lighter, we'll reflect on what God has to say about 'Fun'. What is real fun? Why does it matter? And how can we enjoy ourselves in a godly way? Then, finally, our series on 'Discipline' will get us thinking about why discipline matters and why it's really good for us!

Enjoy!
The *Mettle* Team

JESUS

FULLY MAN + FULLY GOD

TUES 1 MAY

IN THIS SERIES on 'Jesus, fully man and fully God', we'll find out more about exactly who Jesus is, what He does and has already done and just what makes Him so incredible. As we come to understand Jesus better, we're inspired to worship Him and live for Him. Let's begin by focusing on some of the names and titles given to Jesus and ways in which He is described. The first of these is the title 'God incarnate'.

READING: Colossians 2:6–12

> 'For in Christ lives all the fullness of God in a human body.'

KEY VERSE V9

TUES 1 MAY

What is the difference between 'chilli' and 'chilli con carne'? 'Chilli' is a spicy vegetable whereas 'chilli con carne' is a savoury dish, often eaten with rice or tortilla – and the main difference between them is the meat. The word 'carne' (flesh) is the Latin word from which we get the words 'incarnate' and 'incarnation'. When we talk about the incarnation of Christ, we are basically saying that Jesus is God with meat: God with skin on, God in the flesh, God in a human body like ours. He is a God-man or man-God.

These verses in Colossians clearly state that the 'fullness' of God lives in Jesus. Not just a bit of God or half of God but all of God living in a human being! If Jesus were not God, but just a good man, then His death would be nothing more than the tragic execution of an innocent man. However, the founder of our faith was more than a man, an historical figure or a famous person: He is God with skin on!

PRAY

Thank You, Lord, for stepping out of heaven and becoming a human being. Thank You for walking the earth in a human body and finding out what it's actually like to be human. Thank You for identifying with me. You're amazing, Jesus, and I worship You.

READING: John 1:1–14

'In the beginning the Word already existed. The Word was with God, and the Word was God.'

KEY VERSE v1

WED 2 MAY

CHALLENGE

God wants to communicate with us today. Dedicate yourself to reading the Bible, as well as to praying and listening to the 'Word' of God this week. Go for it! God really wants to communicate with you!

It is now possible to talk 24 hours a day, 7 days a week. We phone, text, use social networking sites, chat rooms, MSN and Skype – and occasionally actually meet the person we are talking to, face to face. All these forms of communication use words, written or spoken, to enable us to converse with each other.

God loves to communicate with His creation. It's interesting that the Bible names Jesus the 'Word' of God. He isn't called the picture of God or the vision of God (or even the book of God) but the *WORD* of God. This name enables us to understand Jesus' mission on our planet: to communicate with and die for His creation. In the Bible we can read the words Jesus said; we can learn about the life He led and the people He touched during His life here on earth.

It's fascinating to note that the Bible tells us that Jesus, the 'Word', was present at the very beginning of creation. This 'Word', Jesus, was with God the Father at the creation of the world before He became a human (John 1:1). We have an eternal God who later became a man (through His incarnation) to communicate the Father's love for us. Amazing!

READING: John 5:18–25

KEY VERSE v18

'For he not only broke the Sabbath, he called God his Father, thereby making himself equal with God.'

Have you ever heard the words: 'Oh, he looks just like his mother!'? Or have you ever caught yourself saying something just like your parents? Whether we like it or not, we all resemble our parents in some way.

According to www.bibletoday.com, the term *Son of God* appears 47 times in the New Testament. The word 'son' here has a very different meaning from our use of the word 'son'. We would say that a son is born to a family but is a completely separate person, with his own identity. The biblical meaning of the word 'son' is that the person bears a resemblance to the father. The Bible tells us that the Jews are sons of Abraham (Acts 13:26). These are not sons by birth, but by resemblance and association. The Jews are sons of Abraham by race and religion; they are not all *biologically* related to Abraham.

In the same way Jesus, the *Son of God*, is not less than God or even 'God part b' but is like God in every way, because He is God. He is God with skin on (incarnate), born to communicate with us (as the 'Word'). Jesus resembles God completely.

THURS 3 MAY

THINK

Do we resemble our heavenly Father in our thoughts and our deeds? How can we imitate Jesus' character as the perfect Son? How can we show others, by our lives, that we are related to God?

READING: Matthew 1:18–25

'... you are to name him Jesus, for he will save his people from their sins.'

KEY VERSE v21

FRI 4 MAY

The fishing trip was nearly over. As the rods, reels and bait were collected up, Chris slipped from the bank and plunged into the lake. He immediately started to cough and splutter and the weight of his clothes pulled him down into the murky water. What Chris needed was a saviour: one who could swim – a trained lifeguard willing to jump into the lake to pull him out.

The very name Jesus means Saviour. Jesus came to earth with the express purpose of saving us from our sins. In the same way that Chris needed a qualified saviour (a lifeguard), we also need a Saviour who is qualified to save us from our sins.

If Jesus were just a mere human being, He wouldn't have been able to save us from our sins. If He were a good man, who helped people and said a few amazing things, He still could not have saved us from our sins. However, because Jesus was perfect and sinless, He was qualified to be our Saviour. His death on the cross 'saved' us from our sins, because He took our punishment for us.

Incarnate, Word, Son of God and Saviour. That's our Jesus!

PRAY

Lord, thank You for the names that have been given to You. Thank You that You became a man who came to communicate with us; thank You that You resemble God completely and shared in our humanity, yet perfectly. Finally, thank You that You saved us from our sins.

READING: John 14:1–10

KEY VERSE v6 — 'Jesus told him, "I am the way, the truth, and the life. No one can come to the Father except through me."'

We now turn our attention this week to some of the names or titles Jesus gives Himself. The best-known of these are the 'I am' sayings.

Firstly, we need to understand that the title 'I am' was used by God when Moses stood before the burning bush. God told Moses: 'I am the God of your father – the God of Abraham, the God of Isaac, and the God of Jacob' (Exod. 3:6). What God was saying to Moses was that before his most distant relatives were born (Abraham, Isaac and Jacob), God existed. He was also showing what a faithful God He had been to them. God continues by telling Moses that He knows of the Israelites' present troubles under Pharaoh and that – through Moses' leadership – He will rescue them from slavery and bring them into the promised land (Exod. 3:7–10).

CONTINUED ▶

WEEKEND 5/6 MAY

WEEKEND 5/6 MAY

Jesus uses the same phrase, 'I am', but adds to it seven words to describe Himself. Today's 'I am' is *the way, the truth and the life*.

Firstly, Jesus comes to point the way to God. Unlike some mystic religions where the emphasis is on self-discovery, Jesus provides us with a way – a way to live, a way to receive forgiveness for sins and a way to get to heaven.

Secondly, Jesus provides us with the truth. In a world full of spin and advertising, Jesus comes to tell us the truth because He *IS* the truth.

And finally, Jesus comes to give us life: life now in all its fullness (John 10:10) and life eternally.

CHALLENGE

Meditate on these words of Jesus. Are you following His way? Do you know that Jesus is true? Are you confident that Jesus gives us a full life now and in the life to come?

READING: John 10:10–21

KEY VERSE v11

'I am the good shepherd. The good shepherd sacrifices his life for the sheep.'

You only have to ask children who is 'good' at something and they'll tell you exactly who's best at football, spellings and drawing. It's important for them to know who's good at something and who isn't.

Here we see Jesus describing Himself as a 'good shepherd'. In Jesus' day a shepherd's job was a lowly occupation, often badly paid, which involved sleeping on the hillside and protecting the sheep from predators. The sheep were wayward, often wandering off and getting lost or into trouble. A bad shepherd would be lazy and would not bother to find the lost sheep; a bad shepherd would run away when faced with danger.

A good shepherd knows the sheep and the sheep know him (John 10:14). He is not a hired hand but the owner of the sheep – and he lays down his life for them (John 10:11).

For human beings to be described as *sheep* is really fitting: we are wayward, often following the crowd, getting lost and into danger. A *good shepherd* is an excellent description of Jesus. He is One who knows and loves us; One who rescues and cares for us; and One who lays down His life for us.

MON 7 MAY

PRAY

Thank You, Jesus, that You are my 'Good Shepherd'; One who knows me personally, and One who lays down His life for me!

READING: John 8:12–19

'Jesus ... said, "I am the light of the world. If you follow me, you won't have to walk in darkness ..."'

KEY VERSE v12

TUES 8 MAY

As a family we often take our holiday in Aberdeen. One of our favourite trips is to the lighthouse on the edge of the busy harbour. It stands 70 feet tall and lights up the bay, guiding many oil tankers and fishing boats safely into the dock. At night, the lighthouse comes into its own, its strong beam streaming across the bay, picking out rocks, sandbanks and other hazards.

Jesus describes Himself as the 'light of the world' and, like the lighthouse, He shows us how to live, by shedding light on our paths. The 'light' Jesus gives helps us not to 'walk in darkness'; it leads us to 'life'. It doesn't force us to live in the light but shows us the way to live. It's up to us whether we choose to walk in that light or stay in the shadows.

William Holman Hunt painted a famous picture called *Light of the World* that shows Jesus holding a lamp and knocking on the door of our hearts. The door has no handle on the outside and can only be opened from within.

In the same way, it's our choice: to walk in darkness or to follow the *light* of life.

THINK

Are you living in the light of Jesus, following this 'light of life', or are you choosing to live in the darkness or the half-light? Perhaps part of your life is not yet fully submitted to God. Take time today to come into the full light of Jesus through honest, private prayer.

READING: John 15:1–4

KEY VERSE v1

'I am the true grapevine, and my Father is the gardener.'

Have you ever seen grapevines in the dead of winter? Often they are cut right back to the wooded stump and, to the untrained eye, look as dead as dead can be. Yet visit that same grapevine in the height of summer and you'll see a full canopy of greenery with dangling bunches of grapes.

This bumper harvest is only possible because of the pruning that has taken place in the autumn. If the vine were left to wither and die, the frost would get into it and kill the whole plant. Only by having its branches cut back will the vine eventually produce quality fruit.

Jesus describes Himself as the 'true grapevine' – the life source of the canopy of greenery and the bunches of grapes. He describes God as 'the gardener', who prunes fruit-bearing branches and cuts off branches that don't produce grapes.

As a farmer carefully prunes the vine, God carefully prunes our lives, cutting off the dead wood that hinders our love and service for Him. If we remain close to Jesus, receiving His love, this painful pruning will enable us to continue to produce good fruit in our lives.

WED 9 MAY

CHALLENGE

Are there areas of your life that need to be pruned? What are the hindrances to God effectively working through you? Are you willing to undergo this painful pruning to allow God, as an expert Gardener, to make you more fruitful?

READING: John 6:32–40

'Jesus replied, "I am the bread of life. Whoever comes to me will never be hungry again."'

KEY VERSE v35

THURS 10 MAY

The countdown to Christmas seems to start earlier every year. By September, the shops will be dusting off their decorations and making space for this year's Christmas stock. TV will be churning out the Christmas adverts and we'll be given the same old message, over and over again: *If you have this ... you'll be happy.* But by Boxing Day we'll see how hollow this message is. Batteries will be flat, toys broken, relationships strained, the poor turkey cold – and we will long for life to return to normal.

Jesus describes Himself as bread and drink for those who never want to be hungry or thirsty again! This is not earthly bread that goes stale or earthly drink that runs out, but eternal food and drink that satisfy us forever. We all have a God-shaped hole in our lives that cannot be filled with *things* or *people* – but only with God.

There will always be the next gadget, the next phone and the next games console. There will always be human ambition to own a good car, a nice house or to have exciting holidays. Jesus tells us that all these things will leave us spiritually hungry and thirsty, but the bread and drink He gives will always satisfy.

PRAY
Thank You, Lord, that if we come to You, we will never be hungry or thirsty again. Thank You that You will always satisfy our souls.

READING: John 20:1–18

KEY VERSE v15

'"Dear woman, why are you crying?" Jesus asked her. "Who are you looking for?"'

You can visit the grave of Jimi Hendrix in Renton, Washington. You can visit the grave of Elvis Presley in Graceland. You can even visit the supposed tomb of the apostle Peter in the Vatican City of Rome, but even though there is a church near the supposed site of Jesus' tomb there's no gravestone to read. You can't lay flowers at the tomb of the 'Son of God' because, you know what, He's not there! Jesus rose from the dead after three days.

Before His crucifixion and death, Jesus told Martha that He was 'the resurrection and the life' (John 11:25). Jesus didn't just make this statement – He later proved it by dying, being buried and then rising again from the dead three days later. The tomb was empty! After His death and resurrection Jesus appeared to His disciples and numerous other people on earth.

We can make claims about ourselves, but how many of them are actually true? Jesus said, 'I am the resurrection and the life' – and then went on to prove it. He was not a man of empty words but a God of ultimate power and authority – even over death.

THINK

The bones of Jesus will never be found because Jesus was raised from the dead by the Father, through the power of the Holy Spirit!. There is now a resurrected, perfect human being in heaven: Jesus Christ!

FRI 11 MAY

15

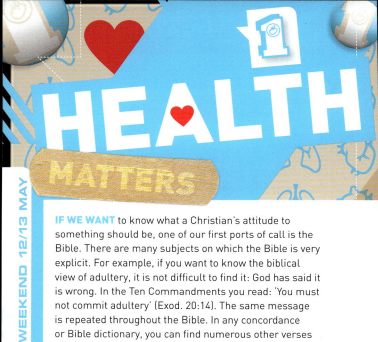

HEALTH MATTERS

WEEKEND 12/13 MAY

IF WE WANT to know what a Christian's attitude to something should be, one of our first ports of call is the Bible. There are many subjects on which the Bible is very explicit. For example, if you want to know the biblical view of adultery, it is not difficult to find it: God has said it is wrong. In the Ten Commandments you read: 'You must not commit adultery' (Exod. 20:14). The same message is repeated throughout the Bible. In any concordance or Bible dictionary, you can find numerous other verses which condemn adultery. It is a fairly clear issue.

But if you want to find out the biblical view of health, it's a bit more complex. When God gave Moses the Ten

READING: 2 Timothy 3:10–17

> 'God uses it to prepare and equip his people to do every good work.'

KEY VERSE v17

WEEKEND 12/13 MAY

Commandments, health was not included. It isn't even included in most church statements of faith. But that's not to say that the Bible can tell us nothing about what our attitude to it should be. Rather, to understand God's view on health we must look for spiritual principles that run throughout the Bible and apply them to this theme.

Over the next two weeks we're going to be thinking about our health. The Bible does have a lot to say about how we treat our bodies, and we'll be exploring this together. We'll think about what can promote or hinder our health and we'll begin to look at exactly what 'health' means: for our minds, bodies and spirits.

PRAY

Father God, thank You that You give us the Bible to teach us and guide us. Please help me, over the next couple of weeks, to understand what a Christian attitude towards my health should be. Amen.

READING: Matthew 22:34–40

'The entire law and all the demands of the prophets are based on these two commandments.'

KEY VERSE v40

MON 14 MAY

THINK

Just as many of the modern rules we encounter have the objective of keeping us and others safe and healthy, how can we see the same principles in the Ten Commandments and the words of Jesus in today's reading?

We live in a world that seems to have hundreds of rules. Teachers, parents and even friends have explicit and unspoken rules that we have to follow. Many of these rules are designed to keep us and others safe and healthy.

In the Old Testament we find hundreds of rules. Following the Ten Commandments in Exodus 20, the books of Leviticus, Numbers and Deuteronomy are stuffed with regulations designed to keep Israel safe and healthy. Today some of these rules seem irrelevant or just plain bizarre!

In our reading Jesus gives us an insight into how we should treat the Old Testament Law today. Our motivation in all things should be to love God and to love our neighbour. If we adopt these aims, we will find ourselves following the laws which are both timeless and the most important of all. For example, if we love God, we'll make time to spend with Him and honour Him in how we use our money. If we love other people, we'll tell them the truth and want to help them, not take advantage of them.

READING: Mark 6:17–32

KEY VERSE v31

'Then Jesus said, "Let's go off by ourselves to a quiet place and rest awhile."'

In our busy lives, it can often be difficult to take time out and rest. If we're not working at something, it can seem wrong somehow – as if we're being lazy. Surely God does not want us to just sit around and do nothing?

But if we take time to look at the Bible accounts of how Jesus lived, we often see that He took time out to rest. Jesus was in high demand. Many people wanted to hear His teachings or to see Him in the hope that He might be able to heal them. He also had to come to terms with the death of John, to whom He'd been very close (see Matthew 14:12–13). But today's key verse shows us that Jesus recognised the importance of looking after His physical health. He and His disciples were not even finding the time to eat, so they had to take time off from their important work to rest and refresh their bodies.

In other passages in the Bible, we read about the importance of rest, refreshment and renewal. Psalm 23 tells us that God 'lets me rest' and 'renews my strength'. Let's not get fooled into thinking that busyness and constant work somehow make God like us more. God wants us to look after ourselves and our physical health.

TUES 15 MAY

THINK

Where in your weekly routine do you find time to rest and renew your body? Do you always take the time to eat properly? Are there any changes you need to make to your weekly routine in order to improve your physical health?

READING: Luke 4:14–21

'He has sent me to proclaim that captives will be released ... the blind will see ... the oppressed will be set free ...'

 KEY VERSE v18

Yesterday we thought about what we could learn from Jesus relating to our health. As well as being concerned with His own health, Jesus shows that He cares about the everyday lives of other people. He isn't just concerned about whether people will go to heaven when they die. He sees their everyday life and concerns as important as well.

In today's reading, Jesus' words highlight that He is interested in the present circumstances of the people He meets. He cares when people are suffering in some way. We know this to be true from the many stories of Him healing people, providing for their physical needs and reaching out to those who are ignored and marginalised.

Jesus is concerned about our eternal salvation. Of course He wants us to turn away from our sins and follow Him. But Jesus is not just concerned about whether or not we will go to heaven. He wants us to have healthy lives here on earth – healthy bodies, minds and souls.

 PRAY

Thank You, Lord, that You care about the situations we find ourselves in every day. Help us to take responsibility for looking after our physical health. Amen.

READING: 1 Corinthians 6:12–20

KEY VERSE v19

'Don't you realize that your body is the temple of the Holy Spirit, who lives in you and was given to you by God?'

It's a fact that our lifestyle choices can have an impact on our health. Many of our modern illnesses can be linked to lifestyle, and we often hear news stories about whether or not smokers should be given lung transplants or alcoholics given liver transplants.

It's helpful in thinking about our lifestyle choices if we do not see our bodies as our own. Rather, they are on loan to us from God – temples for His Holy Spirit. We should therefore think carefully about how we care for our bodies and what we put into them.

I have a precious necklace that was given to me by my great-grandmother before she died. It is over 100 years old and means a great deal to me. I think carefully about where I keep this necklace as I don't want it to become lost, tarnished or broken. The place where I keep it is an important consideration. In the same way, if our bodies are temples where the Holy Spirit lives, then we should keep them fit and healthy. Surely only the best should do!

THURS 17 MAY

CHALLENGE

Reflect on whether there are any aspects of your life that could be healthier. Is your body fit to be a temple where the Holy Spirit can live?

READING: Luke 2:41–52

'Jesus grew in wisdom and in stature and in favor with God and all the people.'

KEY VERSE v52

FRI 18 MAY

In today's Bible reading we learn a bit more about Jesus as a young child growing up. It may be a familiar story to you. The passage ends by explaining that as Jesus grew up, He grew in four areas:

- in wisdom – intellectually
- in stature – physically and in terms of character development
- in favour with God – spiritually
- in favour with people – socially

Similarly, all of us need to develop in those areas in order to be mature and balanced people. If we neglect any one area, then we will be like a four-legged stool or chair with a leg missing – likely to be a bit wobbly!

We often think that God is only concerned with our spiritual growth, but this is simply not the case. We cannot isolate our spirituality from the rest of ourselves as to God (and in Jewish thinking) every part of life is spiritual and significant. Looking after our bodies and ensuring healthy development in other areas is also important. All four of these areas are important and each has an effect on the others. To be healthy, we need to grow intellectually, physically, spiritually and socially, as Jesus did.

THINK

Look again at the four areas in which the young Jesus grew. How are you doing in each of these four areas? Pray that God would help you to develop healthily in each of these.

READING: 1 Timothy 4:11–16

> **KEY VERSE v12**
>
> 'Be an example to all believers in what you say, in the way you live, in your love, your faith, and your purity.'

Think about Christians you admire – they could be your family and friends, people in your church, or someone from the other side of the world. What is it about them that inspires you?

Timothy was a young Christian who was mentored and taught by Paul. Many believe that Timothy ended up co-writing some of Paul's letters and leading a church in Ephesus. Today's reading tells us that instead of always being influenced by others, Paul encourages Timothy to be the one leading the way. Paul challenges Timothy to set an example in the way he lives, in the way he loves others, and in his faith and purity.

We should be encouraged by this passage to examine the way in which we live our lives. Even though we

WEEKEND 19/20 MAY

CONTINUED ▶

might be young, we can still influence those around us. The way we speak and behave affects those who live around us. When we're healthy, we're more likely to be happier, calmer, more patient, and generally the type of person others would like to hang around with.

As young people, peer pressure can be a significant issue. Are you helping to set a trend by looking after all aspects of your health? Do you follow the crowd or are you an example 'in the way you live' (1 Tim. 4:12)? Timothy is also told to 'Keep a close watch on how you live' (1 Tim. 4:16). Think back to the different areas in which we said we should be growing – intellectually, physically and in character development, spiritually and socially. Are you keeping a close watch on how you are developing in all these areas?

CHALLENGE

Mark yourself out of ten on your intellectual, spiritual and social health and character development. Be honest! Are you setting a good example in the way you live?

READING: Proverbs 3:1–8

KEY VERSE v2

'If you do this, you will live many years, and your life will be satisfying.'

Being healthy brings a lot of benefits. For example, healthier people tend to be happier, live longer and play a more active role in society.

In today's reading we are encouraged that if we follow God's way of living then '[we] will live many years, and [our] life will be satisfying' (Prov. 3:2). Have you ever noticed how many Christians often seem more accepting when they go through times of trouble? If we have faith that we are following God's will for us, then we somehow feel more secure, even when things are tough.

And it's not just feeling happier about the situation we're in. By living the way God intended, we are told that we 'will find favor with both God and people, and [we] will earn a good reputation' (Prov. 3:4). What's more, God's way is the way of healing. If we live His way, our bodies will be strengthened too. That's not to say that we'll automatically be fit and healthy, but there is a clear link between spiritual and physical health.

Whilst God does not promise an easy life in return for being a Christian, we know that following God's commands is the wisest and healthiest way to live.

MON 21 MAY

PRAY

Father, help me to follow Your plan for my life. May I develop in the ways You want me to develop, as I seek Your will for me. Amen.

READING: Psalm 139:13–18

'You made all the delicate, inner parts of my body and knit me together in my mother's womb.'

KEY VERSE v13

TUES 22 MAY

Think about something really precious you own. It may be your mobile phone, an iPod, your pet, your car or something else. What do you need to do to make sure that it is well looked after? You probably need to invest time and energy. For example, you may need to charge your phone regularly, make the effort to sync music onto your iPod, play with your pet or clean your car. What happens if you neglect these things?

Today's reading tells us that God created us and gave us incredible bodies that can do amazing things – but we need to look after them. If you look after your mobile phone because it cost a lot, or your pet because you really care about it, how much more should you look after your physical body?

Pretend that you're in a biology lesson for a moment. What does your body need in order to grow and live well? Surely it's worth putting the time and effort into looking after the bodies God has gifted us with.

THINK

Caring for our bodies can be part of our worship of God – how can we make the most of what He has given us and look after it well?

READING: 1 Timothy 4:6–10

'Physical training is good, but training for godliness is much better …'

The Bible talks a lot about being an athlete, using this metaphor to help us understand how we are striving towards a prize in our spiritual lives. Take a look at some of these references:

- Philippians 3:10–14
- 1 Timothy 4:6–12
- 2 Timothy 2:1–5
- 2 Timothy 4:6–8

God is interested in every part of us. We might think of our bodies, minds and spirits as being separate from each other, but they're all very closely connected. In fact they're all part of each other. It is important to remember that what happens in one aspect of our life (eg physical or emotional) can affect the other parts. For example, if we're feeling depressed and have low self-esteem, we can feel physically tired. It can affect the way we relate to God too.

As Christians we want to grow in our relationship with God, but we can't do that in isolation from developing other aspects of our personality and character. We must aim to grow and develop in all areas, including looking after our physical health.

WED 23 MAY

THINK

We can learn a lot from athletes and their dedication to training and developing their skills. If we can apply this dedication to working on our health, we will certainly reap the benefits.

READING: Hebrews 12:1–9

'... let us strip off every weight that slows us down ... And let us run with endurance the race God has set before us.'

KEY VERSE v1

THURS 24 MAY

So often our health is affected by negative things we do, drink or eat. In Hebrews we're challenged to 'strip off every weight that slows us down, especially the sin that so easily trips us up' (Heb. 12:1).

Although the passage is a metaphor for running a spiritual race, this idea also applies to getting rid of anything that could harm our physical health. There may well be things in your lifestyle that you need to change in order to improve your health. Maybe you're always tired because you stay up late watching TV, or perhaps your body isn't as toned as it should be because you're always snacking on chocolate. You may be aware that you haven't been looking after your body as well as you could. Is it time to think about getting rid of some of the old negative habits, and creating some healthier habits? We'll be looking in more detail tomorrow at what changes you might want to make.

PRAY

Father God, help me to recognise ways in which I need to make changes to my lifestyle so that I live more healthily. Amen.

READING: Philippians 3:5–14

KEY VERSE v13

'... I have not achieved it, but I focus on this one thing: Forgetting the past and looking forward to what lies ahead ...'

Yesterday we highlighted the idea that there may be aspects of our physical lifestyle which we need to change. You may already be an accomplished sports person, in which case you probably already have specific targets for your health; or you may have been convinced for the first time that taking care of your body is part of your worship to God.

We read today that Paul is talking about being focused on a future objective and knowing what we want to achieve. Sometimes becoming healthier can be a real challenge, but Paul tells us to look towards the prize of heaven, the prize of becoming all that God intended us to be. Part of this is about being physically healthy, as we have seen.

We will all need to set different targets in regard to our physical health. For some of us this might involve regular exercise; for others it might be to cut down on the amount of junk food we eat or to increase our intake of water. Perhaps for you it is making sure that you get to bed at a decent hour to ensure a good night's sleep.

FRI 25 MAY

CHALLENGE

Spend some time today thinking and praying about how God would have you change your lifestyle to take more care of your physical health. Then make some changes!

FUN
WHAT IS FUN?

'IT'S FUN TO HAVE FUN, but you have to know how.' The Cat in the Hat might have been on to something. The writer of Ecclesiastes would probably agree. Life is hard and often unfair, and it can really get us down if all we do is work. It's important to take time to enjoy life and have fun sometimes. Then again, it's equally important to be wise about how we have fun. A lot of things that sound like fun can actually hurt us or the people around us, and end up making us miserable. We need to think about what we're doing in our quest to enjoy ourselves. 'Having fun' doesn't mean being irresponsible.

READING: Ecclesiastes 8:9–17

'... there is nothing better for people in this world than to eat, drink, and enjoy life.'

KEY VERSE v15

WEEKEND 26/27 MAY

So when should and shouldn't we have fun? Are there limits on what we should do as we try to enjoy life? In fact, what *is* fun? We'll explore all these questions in this series of Bible readings. We'll also investigate what God has to say about fun. God loves to give His people good things, to share His joy with us and to let us enjoy the world around us. As we'll find out, God also loves a good party. But does that mean that 'anything goes' as far as God is concerned? Hmmm. Perhaps not. But more on that later. For now, just be encouraged that having fun is a good thing. How much fun are you having at the moment?

THINK

On a scale of 1–10, how much time do you usually spend having fun? If it's less than 4, make a point of doing something you enjoy today. On the other hand, if it's more than 8, perhaps you should spend a little more time on doing something productive.

READING: Psalm 8:1–9

'... I look at the night sky and see the work of your fingers ...'

KEY VERSE v3

MON 28 MAY

Our world is stunning. God's creation is spectacular. There are so many jaw-dropping sights to see and so much variety. For example, there's the Atacama Desert in South America; the driest place on earth with areas where rain has *never* been recorded! It's dry, but it's certainly beautiful too. There are volcanic rocks, sand dunes and almost always perfect blue skies. At the other end of the scale, perhaps you'd like to visit the Arctic, with its permanent, unspoilt pack ice and winter temperatures which sometimes drop below –50°C. It might not sound inviting, but it does boast the aurora borealis – the famous Northern Lights – a natural and extraordinary light display in the sky. And we haven't even begun to describe the jungles, beaches, mountains and oceans which are out there, waiting to be discovered. God's creation is simply awesome. Discovering it and enjoying it can be one of the most fun and satisfying things you'll ever do. It's not as if we need to go far to make a start, either. Just going to your local park and appreciating the beauty around you can be enough to bring a smile to your face.

PRAY

Thank God for the amazing world He's made. Then get out and explore it! Keep thanking God for the new things He shows you.

READING: Mark 10:13–16

KEY VERSE v14

'For the Kingdom of God belongs to those who are like these children.'

When I turned 30, I decided that I wanted to resist the idea that I was supposed to be old and boring now. So, to celebrate my birthday, I had a childhood regression party. I got together with my friends and we did all sorts of things we used to do when we were kids. We ate jelly and ice cream, guzzled fizzy pop and played Swingball and classic video games. It was great fun and it made me wonder why I don't do that kind of thing more often.

When Jesus says 'the Kingdom of God belongs to those who are like … children', I don't believe He means that we need to be childish to follow Him. However, I do believe Jesus wants us to have a childlike, uncomplicated faith in Him and to appreciate the simple joys of life like children do. We don't have to live on jelly and ice cream, but perhaps we should be open to fun things, even if they're not 'cool'. If we're willing to do that, we can rediscover some of life's simple joys. Maybe that's actually quite a godly thing to do.

TUES 29 MAY

CHALLENGE

Think back to something you really enjoyed doing when you were seven or eight years old. Why not do it again, just for fun?

READING: 1 Samuel 18:1–5

'… Jonathan made a solemn pact with David, because he loved him as he loved himself.'

KEY VERSE v3

WED 30 MAY

You pass an important exam. What do you want to do? Tell someone, I expect. What if you've had a really difficult day? Again, I guess you'd want to talk to someone about it. Or what if the person you fancy asks you out? You'd probably want to tell someone about that pretty soon, too. Whatever's going on in your life, having a friend with you makes things better. When everything's going great, it's good to have a friend to share it with. And, when something's wrong, it makes such a difference to have someone who'll listen to your worries, cheer you up and stick with you.

This was David's experience too. Jonathan wasn't just a casual friend to him; he cared about David deeply and was committed to sticking with him, whatever happened. Jonathan's friendship made David's life just that bit more joyful. And later on, when things really started going wrong for David, Jonathan was still there to help him (see 1 Sam. 20). A true friend makes life better, more joyful and just more fun.

THINK

Think about who your best friend is. Thank God for this person, then think about what you can do to appreciate your friend and make your friendship stronger.

READING: Isaiah 43:1–7

KEY VERSE v1

'Do not be afraid, for I have ransomed you. I have called you by name; you are mine.'

Ever wondered exactly what it is that makes you cringe when your dad tries to be cool? Or what's so ridiculous about a 12-year-old kid smoking? Or why it makes you feel uneasy when a salesman smiles slightly too widely? Well, they're all trying to be something they're not. And when a person does that, it just looks wrong. The trouble is: it's so easy to find ourselves trying to be something we're not. Perhaps you sometimes end up doing something you don't enjoy with your friends, just because they seem to think it's cool.

God created each of us and made us all different – including our sense of fun. So we won't all enjoy the same things. Maybe we should all be just a little braver by being true to who we are and doing whatever *we* enjoy doing. This might mean an awkward conversation with your friends, but then they might surprise you too. My friend John once had to admit to the friends he often went to the pub with that he just didn't like beer. There was a pause, then three or four of the other guys admitted the same thing! Being true to who we really are is a great feeling. It's really liberating, it takes us closer to God's individual plan for us – and it's just more fun that way!

THURS 31 MAY

CHALLENGE

Have you been put off doing something you really enjoy doing because it's just not 'cool'? Be yourself and do it anyway!

READING: Romans 6:20–23

'You are now ashamed of the things you used to do, things that end in eternal doom.'

KEY VERSE v21

FRI 1 JUN

Our actions have consequences. Just ask Charlie. When he was 12, Charlie won a competition at a youth event and was given a big bag of sweets as a prize. Charlie now had a decision to make. He could choose to share his prize with his mates, who were all smiling eagerly and waiting to be offered a sweet or two, or he could just scoff the lot himself. Charlie chose the second option. By the time the event was over, the bag of sweets was empty and Charlie was looking distinctly green. When he got home, Charlie ran upstairs to the bathroom and was noisily sick.

Charlie only wanted to enjoy himself, but he wasn't very wise about how he went about it. He was so focused on having a good time that he didn't think about how his behaviour was damaging him. In Romans, Paul takes this idea a step further. He explains that when we live selfishly, ignoring God and doing our own thing, we're dying inside; destroying ourselves.

There's nothing wrong with having fun, but we mustn't ignore God in our quest for a good time. We might think that life without God means freedom, but it will make us sick. True freedom only comes through following Jesus.

PRAY

If you know that you've been trying so hard to have fun that you've been ignoring God, now would be an excellent time to say sorry and ask God to have His way in your life.

READING: Galatians 5:13–26

| KEY VERSE v13 | 'But don't use your freedom to satisfy your sinful nature.' |

More than a third of under-18s who've been in prison end up committing more crimes when they're released.* Obviously this means that the majority go back to being law-abiding citizens, but that figure is still alarmingly high, don't you think? There have been all sorts of discussions about why this statistic is so high; why people who've been in prison so often end up going back there. There seems to be a general agreement that prisoners often end up becoming 'institutionalised'. That is, they get so used to being in prison that when they're set free, they don't know what to do with themselves. The only life they know is one of crime and prison. Any alternative they can see is frightening to them.

WEEKEND 2/3 JUN

CONTINUED ▶

In today's reading, Paul explains that we were all once prisoners, too. Before we knew Jesus, we were held prisoner by sin. Jesus has set us free from that. He's set us free to know God, live His way and be guided by the Holy Spirit. But there's a problem. We can tend to become 'institutionalised' by sin – so used to instant thrills and living just to please ourselves that we keep going back to doing things we know are wrong. There is an alternative. Instead of going back to the way we lived before we knew Jesus, we can choose to let the Holy Spirit guide us. That's not always easy. It may sometimes look as though we're missing out on some fun. But living God's way brings us joy and peace that we'll never find anywhere else. We're all free, but we must choose what to do with that freedom.

THINK

Are there any bad habits from your old way of living that you keep slipping back into? Jesus can set you free from these things. Ask for His help and talk to a friend you really trust, who can help you and pray for you.†

---

*Source www.justice.gov.uk
†If your habit is linked to an addiction or dependency, there are Christian groups to help. Talk to your pastor or youth leader to find support.

READING: Philippians 2:1–11

KEY VERSE v4

'Don't look out only for your own interests, but take an interest in others, too.'

I hope by now this series of readings has given you the idea that fun is a good thing and that God wants us to enjoy life! But I wonder how good we are at considering the people around us when we're having fun. If we're not careful, our quest to have fun can be selfish – it can blind us to other people's needs. Paul urges us to have the same attitude as Jesus and to put other people first. This includes what we do to enjoy ourselves.

For example, my friends and I always have a dilemma when we go to the cinema. Some of us like action films, some like comedies and some like period dramas. So we always have a big discussion in the foyer of the cinema, negotiating over which film we're going to see. We don't always end up with everyone 100 per cent happy with the choice, but we do try, at least, to bear everyone's tastes in mind. God wants us to enjoy life, but how can we make sure that the people around us are enjoying life too? Fun is good, but it should never be at the expense of other people.

CHALLENGE

Next time you're doing something you enjoy, pause for a minute and think about the impact you're having on the people around you.

READING: 2 Corinthians 1:3–7

'He comforts us in all our troubles so that we can comfort others.'

KEY VERSE v4

TUES 5 JUN

In my final year at university, one of my housemates got dumped by his girlfriend. He was shattered and retreated into himself. We did the best we could to help him through it. We let him talk when he wanted to talk, just spent time with him at other times, and eventually we managed to coax him into coming with us for a night out. In time, he went back to being his old self. I don't always get things like this right, though. A while ago I got the impression that another friend was feeling down, but we'd mostly lost touch and I didn't get around to calling him. A few months later, I finally phoned him and found out that he'd tried to kill himself. I couldn't help but wonder whether I'd have made a difference if I'd spoken to him earlier.

Comforting our friends, doing our best to cheer them up and help them, is important. God is the one who comforts us when we're in trouble, and we should be ready to show the same comfort to other people. Sometimes this means helping our friends forget what's on their mind. At other times it's about listening, being a shoulder to cry on and praying with them. It really matters that our friends know we're there for them. It can help them not just to carry on but to enjoy life.

PRAY

Pray for any of your friends who you know are struggling at the moment. Ask God to show you what you can do to comfort them.

READING: Proverbs 15:28–33

KEY VERSE v30

'A cheerful look brings joy to the heart; good news makes for good health.'

Proverbs is full of wise observations and good advice for real life. Today's reading reminds us that simple things can make a real difference to people around us. Have you ever noticed that when you share some good news with people, it cheers them up? When my wife and I found out that we were expecting a baby, we wanted to tell everyone we knew! We found that it wasn't just us who enjoyed sharing the news; it made our friends happy too. Sharing good news is a sure way to enjoy life, both for you and the people you're sharing it with. It encourages us all and builds us up.

Taking this a step further, what about sharing the best news of all, the good news of Jesus? We know that following Jesus is the best, most satisfying life imaginable, so let's have the courage to tell our friends about Him! This good news will mean that they can enjoy life to the full, for eternity.

CHALLENGE

What good news have you heard recently? If you have a piece of good news, share it! That includes sharing the best news of all.

READING: Job 2:11–13

'Then they sat on the ground with him for seven days and nights ... they saw that his suffering was too great for words.'

KEY VERSE v13

THURS 7 JUN

I have vivid memories of the time when a friend from my church lost his dad. His dad was killed suddenly and violently, and it came as a massive shock to him. All of us in the church did everything we could to support him and his family, but we realised that we couldn't pretend to understand what he was going through. All we could do was to be there for him.

Some things in life are bigger than having a good time. Job's friends drop everything to be with their friend when he's suffering. They don't try to explain away what's going on, they don't attempt to give glib, simplistic answers, and they don't just tell him to cheer up. When something awful happens to someone we know, we can learn from Job's friends. At times like these, we need to just be with our friends, to show them that we haven't forgotten them and neither has God. We need to 'weep with those who weep' (Rom. 12:15). We can leave having fun for another day.

PRAY

Father, thank You for always being with me when I'm suffering. Please help me to show the same commitment to my friends. Amen.

READING: Matthew 5:13–16

KEY VERSE v13

'You are the salt of the earth. But what good is salt if it has lost its flavor?'

Salt adds flavour. It makes food tastier and more interesting. If you've ever eaten chips without seasoning, you'll know how bland they can be and what a difference it makes if you add just a little sprinkling of salt. When Jesus tells us that we are salt, He means that He wants us to add flavour to the world – to make it more godly and more exciting. Those of us who know Jesus should add flavour to the places we go and the people we meet. This includes bringing a sense of fun.

This isn't to say that we should simply try to entertain people, if that's not what we're naturally like. It's about carrying God's Spirit and a sense of His joy into situations. This isn't something we can do in our own strength. If we want to carry God's joy with us, we need to regularly spend time with God, receiving His Spirit, who is the One who gives us joy. So if you're not in the habit of spending time with God, praying, listening and reading the Bible, it's so important to get into that habit. And for all of us, let's spend time with people and ask God to bring them His joy through us.

FRI 8 JUN

PRAY

Thank God for His gift, the Holy Spirit. Ask the Holy Spirit to fill you and give you a sense of His joy to take to other people.

DISCIPLINE
SELF-DISCIPLINE

WEEKEND 9/10 JUN

WHAT BAD HABITS annoy you most? Maybe your dad has a really loud and embarrassing laugh or perhaps your sister leaves her dirty socks lying around the house. Do you have any habits that you know annoy other people? Have you perhaps tried to break your bad habit?

We all have habits. Some of them are good, some are bad, and some are just plain weird! Think about your routines in the morning or evening, either when getting up or going to bed. Do you have to do things in a certain order? For example, I can't have breakfast until after I'm dressed. This is one habit I've got into. My mother has developed a habit in the way she hangs washing on the line – similar items must all be grouped together.

READING: James 2:14–26

'What good is it ... if you say you have faith but don't show it by your actions?'

KEY VERSE v14

WEEKEND 9/10 JUN

I often read about how long it takes to make something a habit. Although it must differ from person to person, many people seem to agree that if you do something repeatedly for three weeks, it starts, at least, to become a habit. We can think of developing habits as developing certain disciplines. We should be purposeful in thinking about which disciplines we want to develop. Having faith in Jesus is great and really important, but sooner or later this faith should affect our words and our actions. Over the next few days we'll be thinking about some of the ways in which our words and actions should change – disciplines we can develop to live in a wiser and more godly way.

PRAY

Lord God, as I think about spiritual disciplines, please show me which habits I should work on and develop. Help me to become more mature and to follow You more closely. Amen.

READING: 2 Timothy 3:10–17

'All Scripture is inspired by God ...
It corrects us when we are wrong
and teaches us to do what is right.'

KEY VERSE v16

MON 11 JUN

CHALLENGE

Reflect again on what you've read today. What might be an appropriate challenge for you in the coming week?

Congratulations! The first discipline we're looking at is Bible study. The very fact that you are reading this shows that you're probably prepared to develop this discipline.

Today's verse points out why this habit is important. The Bible is an important means of God's guidance for us. By studying it, we are allowing God to equip us to become better followers of Him and to fulfil the plans He has for us.

If you don't yet study the Bible every day, challenge yourself to set aside 15–20 minutes to do this and reflect on what you've read. How quickly does it start to become a habit? Think about the time of day when you do this. Are you always in a rush in the morning, struggling to fit it in? Do you find it difficult to stay awake and concentrate just before bed?

If you have already developed the discipline of studying God's Word at a regular point in the day, then think about how you could bring it in at other times as well. For example, maybe you could stick a Bible verse onto your mirror where you will see it often; or set one as a welcome message when you switch on your phone. Try to make God's Word a more central part of your life.

READING: 1 Thessalonians 5:16–24

KEY VERSE v17

'Never stop praying.'

Another key discipline we need to focus on is prayer. There are many different arguments as to why prayer is important and we don't have time to go into them all here. Today's verse makes it clear, though, that prayer is crucial and that it should be a central part of our daily life.

When something significant happens during the day, is your first thought to turn to God in prayer? It may be to ask for help or it may be to thank Him for something. Personally I know that so often I don't think to talk to God about something until later on in the day. My initial reaction is: how can I deal with the situation myself? Or: who can I ring or text about the situation?

As well as prayer being a feature throughout our day, we should also set aside specific time each day to devote to prayer. If you're anything like me then maybe your mind easily wanders during these prayer times. I found that a prayer journal really can help. It helps to focus your thoughts and enables you to look back and see ways in which your prayers have been answered.

TUES 12 JUN

CHALLENGE

Do you pray every day? How often and for how long? Do you give time to listen for a response from God or do you quickly rush on to the next thing after praying? Could you, perhaps, think about starting a prayer journal, as suggested earlier?

READING: Hebrews 10:19–25

'And let us not neglect our meeting together, as some people do, but encourage one another …'

KEY VERSE v25

WED 13 JUN

THINK

Which Christians around you do you respect? Do you allow them to influence your life by meeting with them regularly? How would you respond to discipline from them? What relationships might God be encouraging you to invest more time in?

In today's world, we often have many different opportunities open to us and our lives can be so busy. With school or college work, sports clubs, socialising with friends, part-time jobs etc, it's a wonder that we're able to fit in any involvement with our local church and/or youth group. Attending church and meeting with other Christians can easily slip down our list of priorities. But today's reading reminds us that meeting with other Christians is another important discipline to develop.

When we meet with other Christians, we should be in the habit of encouraging one another and spurring each other on in our faith. Think about who you generally turn to for advice when you need help in making a decision. Do they usually give godly advice? Think too about what happens when people come to you for advice. Do you tell them what you think they want to hear, or do you really think and pray about the advice you give? Proverbs 27:17 tells us that, as friends, we can be instrumental in developing each other. Do you take that seriously in your own relationships?

READING: Colossians 3:16–25

KEY VERSE v23

'Work willingly at whatever you do, as though you were working for the Lord rather than for people.'

Yesterday we thought about how being involved in our local church and spending time with other Christians are important habits to develop. The way in which we serve and give our time and skills for others is another important spiritual discipline. I imagine that you're probably already heavily involved in your church, maybe helping with children's work or in the music group. Today's verse tells us that *everything* we do (not just volunteering at church) should be done as if we are doing it for God.

Perhaps helping at church on a Sunday is already a priority for you. But how do you think about serving God at other times in the week? Are there other opportunities during the week when you could use your time to serve God? Could you offer to babysit so that someone can attend an event at church? Or could you perhaps visit a member of the church who is elderly or unwell?

Even if you don't currently have extra time to spare during the week, think about what does actually occupy your time. Today's Bible verse reminds us that even when we're not obviously serving God in what we're doing, we should do *whatever we do* as if it were for God.

THURS 14 JUN

PRAY

Father, thank You for giving me skills and talents. Please show me how You want me to use these skills, then give me opportunities to do those things. Amen.

READING: 1 Chronicles 16:23–36

'Give to the LORD the glory he deserves ... Worship the LORD in all his holy splendor.'

FRI 15 JUN

THINK

Reflect on your own experiences of worship. Is it a regular part of your life, and not just on a Sunday?

The next spiritual discipline we are going to look at is worship. Worship features throughout the Bible. In Genesis we read of how Cain and Abel made offerings to God (Gen. 4:3–5). We can read and enjoy David's songs of worship in the book of Psalms, and also read about him dancing before the Lord in 2 Samuel (2 Sam. 6:14). We can even find amazing descriptions of worship in Revelation (eg Rev. 19:1–10). And right throughout the Bible there are numerous other examples of people worshipping God.

To worship means to acknowledge how great God is, in both our words and our actions. Worship should not be all about us but should focus on God. Taking part in worship reminds us of who God is and who we are; people created and loved by God.

Because of the wide variety of kinds of worship in the Bible, we should be reminded that there is no one right way to do it. Worship is not just about singing songs at church on a Sunday. Our whole lives should be acts of worship (Rom. 12:1), pointing to God and who He is.

READING: 1 Corinthians 9:24–27

KEY VERSE v27

'I discipline my body like an athlete, training it to do what it should. Otherwise ... I myself might be disqualified.'

Over the weekend we will take a quick break from looking at individual disciplines we should be trying to develop and think more generally about why being disciplined is important.

Some people seem to be remarkably self-disciplined. They manage to complete all their homework on the night they get it, and never leave deadlines hanging over them until the last minute. Unfortunately I'm not organised enough to be like that!

Paul gives us real food for thought in today's key verse. We should be disciplined in training ourselves to do what God wants us to do. If we profess to be Christians and follow Christ, then we must practise what we preach.

Many people are put off Christianity because they see the hypocrisy with which so many so-called 'Christians' live their lives. On the one hand, these 'Christians' talk about a message of peace and forgiveness, but then they gossip nastily about other people. Or, perhaps, they believe that everybody should attend all the church services and youth events on offer, but then they go out and get drunk every Friday night.

Paul likens this kind of behaviour to the risk of being disqualified. What good is it to say that people should live a Christian lifestyle, if we are not seen to make the effort ourselves? When we are seen to live up to the claims we make, then people will respect us and be more interested in what we have to say.

CHALLENGE

Do you need to develop more self-discipline and train yourself further in any aspects of your life? Ask God, as the Master Coach, to help you in your training.

READING: Acts 1:1–11

KEY VERSE v8

'And you will be my witnesses, telling people about me everywhere …'

MON 18 JUN

We're back again to looking at some of the spiritual disciplines we should be developing. Next up, evangelism. The concept of sharing our faith often scares us. But if we truly believe the good news of the gospel, if we catch a glimpse of Jesus and see how amazing He is, surely we will be inspired to share this with other people. Notice how today's key verse uses the word 'will' – evangelism is a command; a compulsion and not an option. Of course, it's as we're filled with the Holy Spirit that evangelism becomes easier and more natural. But, even so, we must choose to take opportunities to share our faith when those opportunities arrive.

Sometimes people go through life wanting the benefits of the Christian life without the challenges. They want a God who loves them and cares about them, but don't want to have to talk about that with somebody else! But the Bible is clear: we need to share our faith with others.

THINK

Most people who become Christians hear the good news through a relationship with a friend. Do you pray for your friends, asking God that they would come to know Him? Do you look for opportunities to talk to them about God?

READING: 1 Corinthians 16:1–4

'On the first day of each week, you should each put aside a portion of the money you have earned.'

KEY VERSE v2

TUES 19 JUN

Today's spiritual discipline is about how we use our money. Throughout the Bible there are a lot of references to money: how we are to use it; how we are to give some to the work of God. As a young person, it can be easy to think that this doesn't really apply to us. However, as we think about the need to form positive habits, it makes sense to start while we are young.

The Bible frequently warns of the dangers of becoming too attached to money and riches. Luke 12:34 says 'Wherever your treasure is, there the desires of your heart will also be.' If we are prepared to give money for God's purposes, then it communicates that He's a priority for us.

Proverbs 3:5 tells us to: 'Trust in the LORD with all your heart; do not depend on your own understanding.' Are we prepared to put our trust in God's ability to provide for us? Do we perhaps think we'll be better off if we can buy a certain new gadget or the latest fashion accessory? Or do we sacrifice our money to God, trusting that He will look after our every need?

PRAY

Thank You, God, that You were willing to sacrifice Your Son for me. Help me to be prepared to give up things for You. In particular, help me to establish the good habit of giving money to You and Your work. Amen.

READING: Matthew 6:16–18

KEY VERSE v16

'And when you fast …'

The last spiritual discipline we'll look at is fasting. Many of us may find fasting the spiritual discipline we struggle with the most. It's certainly the case for me. As with evangelism, however, fasting is not to be seen as optional. Our reading talks about '*when* you fast' not '*if* you fast'.

So why do it? Firstly, going without a meal gives us extra time to spend with God, reminding us, when we feel hungry, to turn to God in prayer instead. It also helps us to depend on God, relying on Him for strength when we find things difficult. Focusing on God rather than food can help us gain a clearer spiritual perspective on life.

But how do we go about it? If you've never fasted before, it's best to start small, perhaps just missing one meal, but drinking water. Make sure someone else knows what you're doing and don't choose a day when you'll need to be very active. If you feel sick, dizzy or faint while you're fasting, stop and eat something. And if you're ill, or you have diabetes, or you sometimes struggle to eat properly, don't go without food – you can fast from other things instead. For example, why not go without TV, caffeine, meat or social networking sites?

*If your parents feel strongly that you should not fast, respect their views. You will have opportunity to do so later in life …

WED 20 JUN

THINK

Have you ever fasted? Why or why not? What do you think might be the benefits of fasting? How could you develop this as one of your spiritual disciplines?

READING: Ecclesiastes 8:9–17

'So I recommend having fun ... there is nothing better for people in this world than to eat, drink, and enjoy life.'

KEY VERSE v15

THURS 21 JUN

Often we think of disciplined people as boring; never able to have fun or be spontaneous. Many people believe that the Christian life has to be like that. But that's just not the case! In today's verse we are told that it is good to enjoy life and have fun.

Being a self-disciplined Christian means that we can go out and have fun, as long as we remain in control of our actions and words. One of my friends at university had a group of friends who regularly went out drinking. He struggled, as a Christian, to know what he should do in this situation. On the one hand, he could refuse to go out with them, risking coming across as dull and boring. On the other hand, he could go out and join in their excessive drinking and drunken behaviour. In the end, he decided that he wanted to show that you could be a Christian and have a good time, without getting drunk. When he went out with them he limited himself to two alcoholic drinks a night. His friends came to really respect his strict two drinks only policy, and many went on to ask him about his Christian faith.

THINK

How do you relate to the non-Christians around you? Are you able to show self-discipline in the way you conduct yourself? How might God want you to alter the way you act around others?

READING: Deuteronomy 6:20–25

KEY VERSE v24

'And the LORD our God commanded us to obey all these decrees ... so he can continue to bless us ...'

Developing spiritual disciplines is rather like an athlete training for an event. Athletes think about all aspects of their lifestyle. As well as physical exercise, they take care to eat the right food, and they avoid drugs and alcohol. In training ourselves to be godly, we need to think about all aspects of our lives. It is no use focusing on just one of the spiritual disciplines. All have a significant part to play in developing godliness.

We may think that we are doing pretty well with our spiritual disciplines. But I've been challenged by the way that athletes do not get complacent and stop working hard. They may be the best, and always come first, but they strive to be even better. There's always something more that could be achieved; another record that could be broken.

Today's reading reminds us that we don't follow God's commands and develop spiritual disciplines just to feel good about ourselves. No, the reward is much greater than that. If we follow God's commands, we open ourselves up to receive all kinds of blessings. What an incentive. Better than any Olympic gold medal!

FRI 22 JUN

PRAY

Lord, please show me the ways in which You would like me to develop. Give me the strength and the self-discipline to become more of the person You want me to be. Amen.

JESUS

FULLY MAN + FULLY GOD

WEEKEND 23/24 JUN

AS WE BEGIN Part Two of 'Jesus, fully man and fully God', we will focus on the humanity of Christ. Beginnings are important. The beginning of a story can tell us a lot about what we can expect to come in the rest of the book. How a person introduces themselves gives us certain impressions of what they're like. The beginning of Jesus' life on earth tells us a lot about Him too. Right from the start, Jesus was just like us: He was born as a baby.

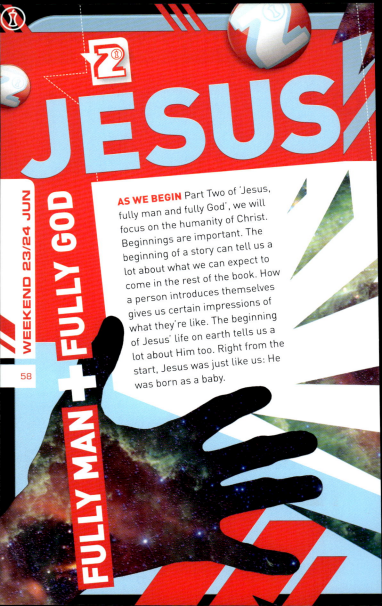

READING: Luke 2:1–7

KEY VERSE v7

'She gave birth to her first child, a son. She wrapped him snugly in strips of cloth and laid him in a manger …'

WEEKEND 23/24 JUN

But, unlike most of us today, He wasn't rushed to hospital in a car or ambulance. He wasn't born in a maternity suite, with doctors, nurses and midwives on hand. There wasn't an incubator available if things got tricky. There wasn't a blood bank somewhere in the hospital if Mary was in need. In reality, things were incredibly basic.

Jesus was born far from home, after days of hard travelling from Nazareth to Bethlehem. There was no room at the inn, so a dirty, smelly stable had to do. There were no new booties and cosy babysuits bought for Jesus, just strips of cloth to wrap around Him to keep off the cold. There was no newly-painted bedroom with cot, mobile and baby monitor; just an animals' feeding trough for a crib.

This was a long way from the throne room of heaven, where angels worshipped Him. God was condensed into the form of a tiny baby. Jesus was completely reliant upon Mary for His every need – a far cry from creation, where Jesus had thrown stars into space!

PRAY

Lord, thank You that You have experienced every part of being human; from birth to death. Thank You that You are now a perfect resurrected human in heaven and yet You are also with me by Your Holy Spirit. You are truly amazing, Lord!

READING: Luke 2:41–52

'When they couldn't find him, they went back to Jerusalem to search for him there.'

 **KEY VERSE v45**

MON 25 JUN

THINK

Although in the eyes of Mary and Joseph He was lost, Jesus was just spending time with His heavenly Father. He didn't run away on purpose. He was simply caught up at the Temple, eagerly questioning the religious leaders. Jesus wanted to learn more about His heavenly Father.

Were you ever lost in a busy shopping centre as a child? Can you remember the feeling of being completely alone, although strangers surrounded you? Can you remember shouting, 'Mum! Dad!' – and they were nowhere to be seen? Did the tears well up? Were you helped by a kind stranger? Can you remember the reaction of your parents when they found you? Were they cross or relieved?

Who would've thought that the earthly parents of the God of the universe would experience the same set of emotions! Jesus was separated from His family – not for a few minutes or an hour, but for three whole days (v.46)! In today's world, Jesus would have been registered as an official missing person, with newspapers and the TV news showing pictures of Him and offering rewards to find Him.

Jesus answered His relieved mother and father by telling them: 'Didn't you know that I must be in my Father's house?' Even as a child, Jesus had a special relationship with His heavenly Father; but He also experienced the same reaction from His relieved parents as we would, if we'd 'gone missing'.

READING: Luke 4:1–13

KEY VERSE v2

'... where he was tempted by the devil for forty days. Jesus ate nothing all that time and became very hungry.'

When we give in to temptation, we can feel guilty and far away from God. We can even feel guilty about being tempted. But struggling with temptation isn't a sin in itself! Jesus experienced extreme temptation from Satan. This passage in Luke shows us three temptations that are common to us all. Firstly, in the area of the weakness of the body. Jesus is hungry after 40 days without food, and Satan turns up at Jesus' weakest point to tempt Him to turn a stone into a loaf of bread (v.3).

Secondly, temptation relating to the weakness of the mind. In an instant Satan shows Jesus the kingdoms of the world and tells Him that they're His if He worships Satan instead of obeying the Father (v.5).

Thirdly, in relation to status. Satan tells Jesus to throw Himself from the Temple so that He can rely upon His status as God's Son and expect God to summon angelic protection for Him (vv.9–11).

Like Jesus, we all are tempted but, unlike Jesus, we frequently give in to temptation. Yet the Bible teaches that none of us is tempted beyond what we can bear (read 1 Corinthians 10:13). God will always provide a way out for us!

TUES 26 JUN

CHALLENGE

When you are feeling tempted, remember the verse from 1 Corinthians. Why not commit it to memory today? Life is full of temptation, but if we hold onto God's promises in His Word we can overcome these challenges.

READING: Luke 4:16–30

'Jumping up, they mobbed him and forced him to the edge of the hill ...'

KEY VERSE v29

WED 27 JUN

Have you ever been in physical danger? Have you ever been in a fight at school? Can you remember the adrenaline kicking in and the 'flight or fight' response coming over you?

Here we see Jesus in very real danger. He is within seconds of being thrown over a high cliff by an angry mob. How would He have felt? What kind of emotions would Jesus have experienced? Fear, anger, confusion, frustration at their lack of understanding?

What was Jesus' crime? Nazareth was His home town: the place where He'd grown up, attended school and worked as a carpenter. Yet here He nearly meets His death! Why? The residents of Nazareth were impressed with His initial speech (v.22) but not with what He went on to say (vv.23–27). Jesus was telling these people that He was the long-awaited Messiah and that Gentiles were just as important as Jews (not a very popular message).

It's so hard to be a Christian around people who really know us well: family, close friends and neighbours. Even Jesus was nearly killed by those who knew Him best.

THINK

Do you struggle with sharing your faith with the people who know you best? Even Jesus wasn't recognised at first by His own people. Take heart though. There's always a reaction (positive or negative) to the good news of Jesus. Our job is to faithfully deliver it, in a loving and sensitive way – and let God do the rest!

READING: Luke 19:41–44

KEY VERSE v41

'But as they came closer to Jerusalem and Jesus saw the city ahead, he began to weep.'

There are a variety of reasons why someone might cry. They might be physically hurt, emotionally upset or moved by the death of a friend (see Jesus' reaction in John 11:35).

Today we see Jesus displaying a very human outpouring of emotion. Like us, Jesus felt deep emotions and He displayed them in the same way. Isaiah calls Jesus 'a man of sorrows, acquainted with deepest grief' (Isa. 53:3), and here we see this prophecy played out in Jesus' earthly life.

However, these tears were not for the death of a friend or due to the agony of Jesus' execution. As He looks down over Jerusalem, Jesus sees a vision of the future of the city. He foretells the judgment of God upon that city whose inhabitants did not recognise who He was or accept His message – and who ultimately sentenced Him to death. It makes Jesus weep.

These verses help us to understand the nature of God. He is not a vengeful, angry God, but One who weeps over a city and its inhabitants. Our God is not some distant cosmic force but a Being who is thinking, feeling and emotional, who weeps over, with and for His children.

THURS 28 JUN

PRAY

Lord Jesus, thank You that You know how we feel and that You understand our human emotions. Thank You that we can go to You in every situation because You understand from experience the feelings we have.

READING: John 11:1–44

'So the two sisters sent a message to Jesus telling him, "Lord, your dear friend is very sick."'

KEY VERSE v3

FRI 29 JUN

PRAY
Thank You, Lord, that You have experienced the full range of human emotions. Thank You that when You were a friend, a brother and a son You experienced the same joy and pain we experience in life.

The majority of songs, films and books are concerned with love. Magazines are full of stories of the rich and famous and their quest for true love. Small children tell their parents: 'I love you, Daddy' or 'I love you, Mummy', when they're being tucked up in bed and read a story. Teenagers waste hours on MSN finding someone to love – and then dropping them for someone else. Our world revolves around love and seems to celebrate what the Beatles sang: 'All you need is love'.

Contrary to *The Da Vinci Code* by Dan Brown, Jesus was never romantically involved with anyone. Nevertheless He did deeply love those closest to Him (disciples, family, friends) with a real bond of brotherly love.

Here we see Jesus' brotherly love for the two sisters, Mary and Martha, and their brother, Lazarus. Just like us, Jesus had strong emotional ties to His friends. When Lazarus died, Jesus wept and was greatly troubled.

Humans are relational beings and are designed to be in relationship with each other and with God (see Genesis 2). As fully human and fully God, Jesus is our example of pure love.

READING: John 15:11–17

KEY VERSE v11

'I have told you these things so that you will be filled with my joy. Yes, your joy will overflow!'

If you look at the established, traditional image of the Church, you don't often think of the word 'joy'. The old church buildings help us to feel reverent but not always full of joy. Yet Jesus was a man full of laughter and joy – so much joy that it 'overflowed' (John 15:11) to those around Him.

The joy Jesus gives us is not silly laughter or giggly humour but a deep-rooted contentment and happiness. Paul tells us that the Spirit of God produces fruit in us and part of this fruit is joy (Gal. 5:22). We can experience joy in any situation. It is not reliant on feelings or emotional reactions to a situation but is the outward expression of a life lived for and with God in the power of the Holy Spirit.

CONTINUED ▶

WEEKEND 30 JUN/1 JUL

Joy is closely linked to peace. If someone is peaceful they are usually very cool and calm in any situation. The psalmist tells us that God is like solid ground under our feet (Psa. 40) and that no matter what may happen to us, we stand firm on that ground of peace and joy.

Jesus had this fruit in His life and it was evident in everything He did. He also wants to give us this same joy – not just a little joy, but so much that we overflow with it.

Are you a contagious Christian? When people look at you do they want to be like you? Are you known as a moaner or as a happy, contented person – no matter what? Do you have this joy that the Spirit gives?

PRAY

Lord, help me to be joyful in my attitudes and in the way I approach life. Help me to be a contagious Christian and to share Your joy with others.

READING: Mark 8:31–37

KEY VERSE v33

'Jesus turned around and looked at his disciples, then reprimanded Peter. "Get away from me, Satan!" he said.'

We all get angry. Sometimes we're wrong to get angry and occasionally we're right. Generally speaking, the angry emotion is not the problem – it's how we handle it.

Today's reading gives one of the few accounts of Jesus visibly responding in anger to a situation. Another significant occasion is when Jesus clears the Temple in anger at the market traders making money from the sacrificial system (John 2:13–20). This time Jesus is reprimanding Peter.

Jesus is angry because Satan is influencing Peter's thinking – Peter does not understand why Jesus has come to earth. He is looking at things from a human perspective. Jesus even goes as far as to speak directly to Satan, who is trying to influence Him through Peter.

Jesus' purpose on earth was to die on the cross for our sins and to point the way back to the Father. Peter is opposing this by looking at things from a worldly viewpoint and not a heavenly one. By contradicting Jesus, Peter is opposing the purposes of God and, therefore, unknowingly working with Satan. This is why Jesus is so angry – not at Peter, but at the opposition to His role as Saviour of the world.

MON 2 JUL

PRAY

Thank You, Lord, that You planned to come to earth as a human to die on a cross for our sins. Thank You that nothing would stop You from fulfilling that purpose, even the words of Your closest friends.

READING: Matthew 26:36–46

'He took Peter and Zebedee's two sons, James and John, and he became anguished and distressed.'

KEY VERSE v37

TUES 3 JUL

As we near the end of Jesus' life we clearly see His humanity in His 'anguish and distress'. No one has experienced the same degree of anguish as Jesus did in Gethsemane that night. We're later told that Jesus sweated blood (Luke 22:44). This condition is called *hematidrosis* and is very rare indeed. Only in cases of extreme stress and acute fear do humans sweat drops of blood.

We are all aware of the suffering Jesus went through on the cross, but before Jesus was arrested and beaten He experienced extreme anguish, stress and fear of sin's destructive and deadly effects. He was preparing for the sorrow and heartache that would be inflicted upon Him on the cross.

Do we understand the extreme agony Jesus endured to bring us out of the darkness of sin and into the light of His forgiveness? This was God, as man, taking our punishment on Himself. It's an incredible, perfect, once-for-all sacrifice!

PRAY

Thank You, Jesus, for Your great sacrifice for me on the cross – for taking away my sin and bringing me into Your light of forgiveness and the promise of eternal life!

READING: Matthew 27:45–56

KEY VERSE v46

'My God, my God, why have you abandoned me?'

As we wind down Part Two of this section on 'Jesus, fully man and fully God', we see that Jesus ends His life like the rest of humankind – in death. Death is the great leveller: however rich or poor, powerful or powerless, beautiful or plain, talented or ordinary, adored or loathed we are, we all die!

Jesus' death on the cross was the ultimate sacrifice for us. It was our sin that held Him to the rough, splintered wood. It was our shame that weighed heavily on His shoulders and, at the point of death, Jesus cried out to His Father; He felt totally abandoned.

Humankind murdered God, its Creator. However, it was to this end that Jesus was born in a smelly stable in Bethlehem. Jesus fulfilled the psalmist's words in Psalm 22 when He hung on the cross. He brought to pass the words of the prophet Isaiah as He endured the suffering that should have been ours (Isa. 53:5).

The act of this 'God–man' dying for us on the cross means that today we can have a relationship with the Father and the forgiveness of our sins through the blood of Jesus.

WED 4 JUL

THINK

Take a flick through some of the days in Parts One and Two and start to reflect on this amazing 'God-man' we worship. He's fully God and fully man; able to identify with us, yet able to offer forgiveness for our sins – because He's the perfect human!

READING: Matthew 28:1–10

'And as they went, Jesus met them and greeted them. And they ran to him, grasped his feet, and worshiped him.'

KEY VERSE v9

THURS 5 JUL

I like a book with a twist in its tale and an ending that really takes you by surprise. Fortunately, the conclusion of yesterday's reading was not the end of the story for Jesus. As most of us will know, He did not stay dead but rose again on the third day. The two Marys saw Him first and their reaction was dramatic: '… they ran to him, grasped his feet, and worshiped him.'

As Christians today, we know that Jesus is alive right now – not as a baby in a manger or a carpenter in His workshop, but in heaven, seated with God the Father. At the time of Jesus' resurrection, however, there were mixed reactions from the disciples. Some, like John and the two Marys, were excited. Some were doubtful – like Thomas who insisted that he wanted to put his fingers into the holes in Jesus' hands and feet before believing. Some were embarrassed, like Peter who'd promised to follow Jesus to the very end, yet had denied Him three times. Meeting the resurrected Jesus forced a reaction from everyone He met.

I wonder what your reaction would be if, today, Jesus appeared to you? What would you do and say? Would you fall at His feet or run?

PRAY

Thank You, Jesus, that Your story didn't end at the cross – there was a twist in the tale. Thank You that You rose again and appeared to many of Your followers before You went to rule at the Father's side in heaven.

READING: Mark 16:14–20

KEY VERSE v19

'When the Lord Jesus had finished talking with them, he was taken up into heaven ...'

In our conclusion to Part Two of 'Jesus, fully man and fully God', we see Jesus doing something that a man doesn't normally do. It's highly unusual for a human being to die, rise again bodily and then be 'taken up into heaven'. This shows Jesus' divine nature as well as His humanity. Jesus' mission was accomplished and He could now reign in heaven with the Father and the Spirit.

Notice that Mark calls Jesus, 'Lord Jesus', in this passage (v.19) to indicate the majesty of Jesus. Also note that Jesus goes 'up into heaven' when He has finished speaking. He had an important mission to explain to His disciples (vv.15–18) before He ascended into heaven.

Finally, look at the disciples' reaction to this unusual sight. They immediately begin to go out and preach everywhere. With words and signs they tell the good news to everyone they meet.

Wouldn't you like to have been there – to have seen Jesus risen from the grave, then lifted up to heaven before your very eyes? No wonder the disciples wanted to tell people about this ... Wouldn't you?

FRI 6 JUL

CHALLENGE

Are you telling people around you about this risen Lord Jesus Christ whom you worship? Why not? It's the best news in the world and we can't keep this life-changing news to ourselves. Jesus has sent us – like His disciples – on a mission!

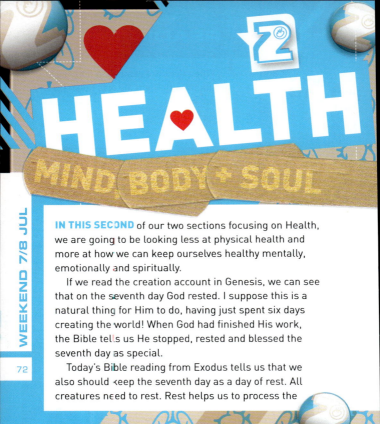

HEALTH
MIND, BODY + SOUL

WEEKEND 7/8 JUL

IN THIS SECOND of our two sections focusing on Health, we are going to be looking less at physical health and more at how we can keep ourselves healthy mentally, emotionally and spiritually.

If we read the creation account in Genesis, we can see that on the seventh day God rested. I suppose this is a natural thing for Him to do, having just spent six days creating the world! When God had finished His work, the Bible tells us He stopped, rested and blessed the seventh day as special.

Today's Bible reading from Exodus tells us that we also should keep the seventh day as a day of rest. All creatures need to rest. Rest helps us to process the

READING: Exodus 31:12–17

'You have six days each week for your ordinary work, but the seventh day must be a Sabbath day of complete rest ...'

KEY VERSE v15

WEEKEND 7/8 JUL

past and prepare ourselves for the coming week. But a Sabbath is more than just a rest, more than just lounging in bed. It's a time to make spiritual space, a time to be thankful to God. The Sabbath can be seen as a taste of what heaven will be like.

When I was younger, Sundays would often be the day when we couldn't go out and play or watch TV, but the Sabbath isn't supposed to be boring and resented. It should be the best day of our week. The punishments for ignoring the Sabbath were so severe because God wanted to underline just how important this regular rest and spiritual space is. It can bring huge benefits to our health and our faith.

CHALLENGE

Have a go at planning your own Sabbath – a time to rest, to be re-energised and to meet with God. Perhaps turn off your phone and resist going on the internet, to give you peace and quiet. Why not go for a walk, or hit the beach and appreciate God's creation?

READING: Matthew 11:25–30

'Then Jesus said, "Come to me, all of you who are weary and carry heavy burdens, and I will give you rest."'

KEY VERSE v28

MON 9 JUL

I loved the feeling I experienced on the last day of school in July, knowing that we didn't have school for the next six weeks. I loved the rest and relaxation that the summer holidays provided. What are the things in our lives from which we need rest? School or work, perhaps – or difficult situations with our family and friends? Think for a moment about those things from which you need a rest.

In today's reading, Jesus offers rest to those who are weary and burdened. What does He say we have to do to find rest? He knows about the concerns that weigh on us, and He offers us rest from them – if we are prepared to come to Him. This means being honest with Him about ourselves – and being prepared to say sorry for the things we've done wrong.

The people to whom Jesus was talking would have recognised the phrase about taking His yoke upon them. The Jewish teachers would talk about taking the yoke of the law – for the Jews had many rules and regulations which they were expected to keep. These laws were a heavy burden to bear. In contrast, Jesus tells us that His burden is light.

THINK

Think again about your burdens. Are these concerns that you are prepared to place before God? If so, why not pray, asking Jesus to give you the rest He promises.

READING: Leviticus 25:1–7

KEY VERSE v2

'... the land itself must observe a Sabbath rest before the LORD every seventh year.'

A couple of days ago we looked at the command to take a Sabbath day of rest. Today's reading tells us that it is not just people who need rest. God says that even the land should be rested from the work of providing food for His people. How many examples of things needing rest (or not being used continually without a break) can you think of? What happens to these things if they do not get their rest?

We often think of rest as an absence of activity. This may lead us to think that it is a waste of time! But everything, including us, needs rest in order to be productive. When we're well rested, we're more effective in our work and our relationships and also more effective as followers of Jesus.

For Christians, rest is an opportunity to catch up with God and to be refreshed by Him. If we neglect this opportunity, we may find ourselves not only physically but spiritually exhausted.

Resting when we need to is not lazy – although some people may think it so. Anyone who deprived themselves of food for long periods would be seen as taking dangerous risks with their health. And yet we will often deny ourselves rest.

THINK

Do you get enough time to rest and be with God? What pressures prevent us from doing this? How could we make sure that we take enough time out to rest and be renewed by God?

TUES 10 JUL

READING: Philippians 4:4–9

'Fix your thoughts on what is true, and honorable, and right, and pure, and lovely, and admirable.'

KEY VERSE v8

WED 11 JUL

CHALLENGE

Take time to confess any inappropriate and sinful thoughts to God. Ask that He would cleanse your mind.

Think about all the things you do to keep your body healthy. Some of those things might include eating the right foods, doing exercise or wearing particular kit, like a cycle helmet, to protect you. But what do you do to keep your mind healthy? If you're like me then that's probably not something you really think about – except when I was revising for exams I was always told to eat more fish to help my brain!

In a similar way to our bodies, our minds can be healthy or unhealthy. Not only that, but the Bible tells us that, as Christians, our spiritual health depends on us having strong, God-focused minds.

In today's reading the apostle Paul teaches us that being pure in our thoughts is crucial for our spiritual health. The thoughts in our minds should be godly thoughts. Romans 8:5 takes this one step further, telling us: 'Those who are dominated by the sinful nature think about sinful things, but those who are controlled by the Holy Spirit think about things that please the Spirit.' There is a link between our lifestyle and our thoughts. When your mind wanders, what kind of thoughts do you find yourself thinking? What might this say about you?

READING: Ephesians 4:17–32

KEY VERSE v23

'Instead, let the Spirit renew your thoughts and attitudes.'

Yesterday we learnt how it is important to not just keep our body healthy but to think about our mind as well. Paul explains in Ephesians 4:22–23 that our mental health should include 'throw[ing] off your old sinful nature and your former way of life' and 'let[ting] the Spirit renew your thoughts and attitudes'.

As we get closer to God, our thoughts and attitudes should change. Think about what you fill your mind with. What do you watch, read and listen to? How have your thoughts and attitudes developed in the past year or two?

In Colossians 3:2 we're called to: 'Think about the things of heaven, not the things of earth.' This doesn't mean that we should only think about going to heaven when we die and ignore the world we're living in now. But we should keep in mind that God's ways are often different from the ways people around us will do things. We should stand out through living God's way.

The best way to protect our minds is to keep them fixed on God and to try to develop Christlike patterns of thinking. We're not being asked to live in a Christian bubble, but we're called to be distinctive – to be salt and light in this world.

THINK — THURS 12 JUL

In what ways could you and your friends support each other in developing healthy minds?

-
-
-
-
-

READING: Matthew 5:1–12

'Be happy about it! Be very glad! For a great reward awaits you in heaven.'

KEY VERSE v12

Today I want us to think about healthy emotions. When life seems hard or unfair, it's natural to feel upset or angry. In fact, it's healthy to express sadness or anger, as long as we do this constructively, rather than lashing out at people around us. But, even if we're struggling with a really difficult situation, we can still choose how to respond to it. Jesus experienced pain, suffering, rejection and persecution, but knew that God was still in control in these painful experiences. So Jesus challenges us to keep this truth in mind: to trust God and thank Him for who He is and what He does, no matter what we're going through.

For someone like me who worries a lot, this is a real challenge! I find it all too easy to dwell on problems, going over and over them in my mind. Someone once compared worrying to sitting in a rocking chair: it gives you something to do, but it doesn't get you anywhere! On the other hand, if we commit our troubles to God and choose to praise Him, we can know His peace and His joy, even in our suffering. We might not always be able to control our emotions, but we can choose how to respond in a healthy way.

PRAY

Father God, help me to always trust in You, however I'm feeling. Help me to remember to be thankful for Your love and goodness, even in times of trouble, and grant me Your peace in difficult situations. Amen.

READING: 1 Kings 19:1–21

KEY VERSE v4

'He sat down under a solitary broom tree and prayed that he might die. "I have had enough, LORD," he said.'

Sometimes life just feels like it's too much. This weekend we're going to look at a Bible hero who felt like giving up and just wanted to die. Elijah had just won an amazing victory with God against the prophets of Baal. These prophets were supported by Queen Jezebel and there were 450 of them and only one of Elijah. All day the prophets had struggled to get their god to light the fire on the altar they had built, but with no success. Elijah, on the other hand, built an altar for God, then drenched it with water, said a simple prayer to God and the whole thing was ablaze.

How excited Elijah must have felt. But just a few hours later we find him in a completely different frame of mind. Elijah would have been exhausted; he'd

WEEKEND 14/15 JULY

CONTINUED

been through so much and would now have felt alone, frightened and extremely vulnerable.

In today's reading we see how God meets Elijah in his depression and helps him back to a healthy mindset. Read it again, pausing at the following verses, and see what God does for Elijah:

- Verses 5–7 – God lets Elijah sleep and provides him with food.
- Verse 13 – God meets with Elijah, who is able to tell Him all that is troubling him.
- Verses 15–17 – God gives Elijah a new mission.
- Verse 18 – God reassures Elijah that he is not alone.
- Verses 19–21 – Elijah is provided with a friend and assistant.

THINK

At those times when you feel low you might find it helpful to ask yourself whether you are simply in need of a good meal, more sleep or, perhaps, a friend to talk to. Spend some time thinking about different people who can help you in challenging circumstances.

READING: Ephesians 6:10–12

KEY VERSE v11

'Put on all of God's armor so that you will be able to stand firm against all strategies of the devil.'

As well as thinking about how we look after our physical and mental health, we should also take care to guard our spiritual health. Just as we need to look after our physical bodies correctly in order that they might grow and develop in the right ways, we also need to care for our spiritual health so that we can grow and deepen our faith further.

When soldiers go to war, they think carefully about what they are wearing in order to give their bodies greater protection. Similarly, in many sports, the clothing and other items worn by participants (eg shin pads, mouth guards, helmets) ensure that the body is well protected from the stresses and strains it might endure. In Ephesians 6 we read about the armour of God; things we should put on in order to protect ourselves from the devil's attacks. Over the next few days we'll be looking in more detail at what the armour of God is and how we can put it on and use it.

THINK

What does it look like when the powers of darkness attack someone? Can you think of examples of when the enemy has tried to attack you in your own life? What might be the consequences of these attacks?

MON 16 JUL

READING: Ephesians 6:13–17

'Therefore, put on every piece of God's armor so you will be able to resist the enemy in the time of evil.'

KEY VERSE v13

TUES 17 JUL

Have you ever gone out dressed in completely the wrong outfit, given the weather or the activity you're about to do? You can be sure that I'll take my coat with me every dry and hot day during the summer but, as soon as it starts to rain, that'll be the day I've left my coat behind.

Many items in the armour of God relate to preparing ourselves spiritually for any attack. Attacks from the devil can come at any time and in any place. We should never find ourselves inadequately prepared. So, what should we do? Much of what we read in today's verses points towards the need to know and really trust in the gospel message.

We need to be familiar with what the gospel message actually is and what it means for us. Regular Bible study is one of the best ways of putting on much of this armour. Do we know the truth of the gospel inside out? Do we put our faith in this truth 100 per cent? Do we lean on God when things are tough, or do we easily forget Him and rely on our own strength? In standing up to the enemy's schemes, there is no better shield with which we can equip ourselves than faith in God.

PRAY

Help me, Lord God, to be prepared for attacks from the devil. Help me to be sure of the truth of the gospel and to have faith in Your protection. Amen.

READING: Ephesians 6:17–20

KEY VERSE v17

'... take the sword of the Spirit, which is the word of God.'

A few years ago I had an attack of ants in my kitchen. At the time I did not have any ant poison to deal with this unwelcome invasion. I looked on the internet for alternative solutions and one thing I remember trying was laying bay leaves all around the kitchen work surfaces. Although the bay leaves made an effective obstacle course for the ants to navigate, the ants didn't seem too bothered. In the end, the only solution was to find some proper ant poison.

Part of being prepared for battle is carrying the right weapon. Today's key verse says that, when we put on the armour of God, the weapon we should be equipped with is God's Word. The use of this weapon is demonstrated by Jesus Himself when faced with the devil. (You can read about this in Matthew 4.) Every time Jesus was tempted by the devil, He quoted Scripture at him.

I know a number of people who memorise specific verses from the Bible which they can say aloud when they are going through a difficult time or a period of temptation. It's great to encourage ourselves with these truths and, because the Word of God is the truth, there is very little the devil can do to attack against it.

WED 18 JUL

CHALLENGE

Is there a verse in Scripture that you could memorise to help you as a weapon when you face attacks from the devil? Why not try a verse like James 4:7?

READING: Genesis 1:26–31

'Then God said, "Let us make human beings in our image, to be like ourselves."'

 **KEY VERSE v26**

We should care about our health because all of life is God's domain. Right from the start of the Bible we see that God is a Creator God. And we are created in the image of God.

In God's design there is an integration of life's different components that cannot be separated from one another. In the same way that the different parts of God's creation need one another to function fully, so we have been created so that mind, body and soul work together as an integrated unit.

If we want to find out more about a person's life we ask questions about their school, their job, their home, their friends, their health, their social activities (such as sport) and other aspects of their life. There is a strong relationship between these different components. Our education can affect what job we can get, which can affect our financial status, and so on. Try as we might, it is impossible to live a compartmentalised life. Issues in one part of life always impact the rest of who we are.

THURS 19 JUL

THINK

Think about all the different aspects of your life. Are you prepared to give them all to Christ or are there certain aspects that you don't think He's bothered about? Ask Him to help you to understand how much He cares about every detail of your life.

READING: Romans 12:1–5

KEY VERSE v1

'... give your bodies to God because of all he has done for you. Let them be a living and holy sacrifice ...'

Right up until Jesus' time, people would regularly take things (usually animals) to the Temple to be sacrificed to God. They would do this to ask for God's forgiveness, to thank Him, or for many other reasons. The priest at the Temple would take the animal from the person who brought it, tear it apart, sprinkle the blood on the altar and then finally put what was left of the sacrifice on the altar and burn it. I'm telling you all this to explain that 'sacrificing' ourselves to God is a serious business. When you sacrifice something, you give up all control and let God do what He likes with it.

Sacrificing ourselves is a scary thing to do, but we know that God loves us and wants what's best for us. He wants us to commit our bodies to Him and also our minds and our wills (v.2), because His plans for us are always best. We should give ourselves to God as a *living* sacrifice (v.1). He's not going to tear us apart, burn us up and destroy us! As we give God control of our lives, we will find that we are truly living, in all aspects of our lives. We will find true and lasting health, for our bodies, our minds and our spirits, if we commit ourselves to God.

FRI 20 JUL

CHALLENGE

Choose to offer yourself to God as a living sacrifice. Commit every area of your life to Him. It might be scary, but it's by far the healthiest way to live.

FUN

FUN FOLLOWING JESUS

WEEKEND 21/22 JUL

I WAS HELPING a group of friends to organise a worship event for our church. We wanted to do a few things that were different from the conventional sung worship. We particularly wanted to help people reflect and thank God for the good things He gives us. So we hit on the idea on serving 99 Flakes (ice creams in cones with chocolate flakes in the top). It might sound silly, but it turned out to be really powerful. People remarked on how long it had been since they'd eaten a 99 Flake, how much it cheered them up and how well it reminded them of all the good things God had given them.

READING: John 10:6–16

KEY VERSE v10

'My purpose is to give them a rich and satisfying life.'

God does give us so many good things. He loves to give us a life that's rich, satisfying and, yes, fun. In this series, we've already unpacked a few principles for a fun and healthy lifestyle, but knowing God should be fun too. God brings us a sense of joy, peace and purpose we can't get any other way. God is also the One who created laughter. Not very many people would automatically associate Christians with fun but, if anything, we should be known as the people who have more fun and more joy in them than anyone else in the world! Does that mean following Jesus will give us an easy life, with no problems and endless, uncomplicated fun? Of course not. But, even when life is hard, it's a rich and satisfying life. And God can give us a deep joy even when we don't seem to have much to be happy about.

Over the next couple of weeks, we'll be looking more closely at the joy God gives us and exactly how following Jesus can be fun.

WEEKEND 21/22 JUL

THINK
What does a 'rich and satisfying life' mean to you? What good things has God given you that you should be thankful for?

READING: Deuteronomy 14:22–29

'When you arrive ... feast there in the presence of the LORD your God and celebrate with your household.'

KEY VERSE v26

MON 23 JUL

THINK

What do you and your friends have that you can thank God for? How can you celebrate this together?

God loves a party! In the Old Testament Law books, God gives very detailed instructions on offerings the Israelites should give and festivals they should mark as acts of worship. This meant far more than dry, religious ceremonies though. Worship was a crucial part of the Israelites' lifestyle, but the way God plans this worship makes it inseparable from celebration. For example, this passage from Deuteronomy tells the Israelites exactly what they should give God from their harvest, but it's far more than just paying some kind of tax. God also tells them to feast and have fun!

What we can learn from this is that God wants His people to enjoy themselves. Of course, it's important to take worshipping God seriously. It's important to get into a habit of giving some of what we have to support God's work, too. But knowing God and worshipping Him doesn't mean that we can't have a good party every now and then. Far from it! When something good happens, let's thank God for it and celebrate.

READING: John 2:1–12

KEY VERSE v10

'A host always serves the best wine first," he said ... "But you have kept the best until now!"'

Christians have a variety of views on drinking alcohol. Some would say it's OK in moderation. Others think we should steer clear of it altogether. However, in Jesus' culture, it was normal to drink wine, at least in moderation. (Perhaps we should bear in mind that it was often safer to drink wine than water, though!) At a wedding, it was particularly important to have lots of wine available. In fact, it was seriously embarrassing for you as the host if you ran out of wine in the middle of the party.

When Jesus turns the water into wine at this party, He is saving the blushes of the host. He's also providing an abundance – gallons and gallons of top quality wine – for thirsty wedding guests. More significant for us, Jesus' actions say something symbolic about how He offers a new, exciting, joyful way of living. Jesus gives us joy, love and peace by the bucket load and it's the best quality of life we could imagine.

TUES 24 JUL

PRAY

Jesus wants to make your life more joyful and satisfying. Ask Him to fill you with His Spirit of joy, now.

READING: Luke 15:11–32

'We had to celebrate this happy day. For your brother was dead and has come back to life!'

KEY VERSE v32

WED 26 JUL

I was 14. I was hanging out with my friends, and we were bored. To pass the time, we were in the garden, seeing who could throw a stone the furthest. When it came to my turn, I watched as my stone went sailing over the wall at the end of the garden and then listened with horror as I heard it crashing through the greenhouse on the other side of the wall. The owner of the greenhouse soon stormed around to our front door, demanding to know who'd damaged his property and leaving me in no doubt that he'd do me some serious damage if I owned up.

God isn't like that greenhouse owner. When we mess up, He isn't waiting to punish us and make us suffer. He just longs for us to come back to Him. When the younger son in Jesus' story comes home, his dad doesn't shout at him, ignore him or tell him how disappointed he is. In Jesus' culture, someone who had disgraced his family like the son had would probably have been executed (see Exodus 21:17). But this father doesn't punish his son. He throws a party instead! What a wonderful picture of God's love for us. If we do something wrong and turn back to Him, He wants to celebrate us being back where we belong.

CHALLENGE

Have you been keeping away from God because you've done something you know was wrong? Turn back to Him now. He's not waiting to punish you. He wants to forgive you and celebrate you being home again.

READING: Psalm 16:1–11

KEY VERSE v11

'You will show me the way of life, granting me ... the pleasures of living with you forever.'

I have a history of buying terrible cars. One particularly unwise purchase broke down the first time I drove it. Having just paid for the car, I then had to pay another £300 to get it fixed. Even the first car I owned, which I loved and which had generally been reliable, had to be scrapped in the end. The engine developed the (rather bizarre) habit of cutting out every time I tried to turn a corner.

Lots of things in life seem fun and reliable now but will break down, fade away, run out or disappoint us in some other way later. Parties come to an end. Money is limited. Stuff we buy breaks. Lots of drink gives us a hangover. Even friends aren't always as loyal as we'd like. But the joy God offers lasts. God's joy always stays with us and never wears out. It goes on forever – into eternity. The only catch is that we'll only know 'the pleasures of living with [God] forever' if we let Him 'show [us] the way of life'. We'll only know God's joy if we're willing to follow Him.

THINK

Are you relying on things that won't last to help you enjoy life? We can have lasting joy in God's presence, but we need to be willing to let Him show us the way to live and then follow Him.

READING: 1 Peter 1:3–9

'There is wonderful joy ahead, even though you have to endure many trials for a little while.'

KEY VERSE v6

FRI 27 JUL

My wife once spent some time in Sierra Leone, helping with a programme that provided healthcare for people who otherwise would have no way of getting it. The country was recovering from a terrible civil war, which had ended only two years previously. There was hardly anyone in the country who hadn't lost someone they loved in the war, or been physically maimed or emotionally scarred by what had happened. But, at the same time, my wife was amazed at how joyful the people she met seemed to be. She got to know one particular woman who came to the clinic. When my wife asked her how she managed to be so joyful when she was so poor and she'd experienced so much pain, the woman's reply was incredible: 'We can't be miserable,' she said. 'If we're miserable, that means the devil has won.'

We all know that life can be hard. But however hard life gets, we still have God's joy in us to help us through. So let's choose to hold on to that joy, even when there are lots of trials to face. Better still, we can look forward to wonderful, perfect joy in heaven, when we'll be free from trials and we'll see God face to face.

PRAY

Thank God for the joy He gives you now and for the perfect joy that's waiting for you in eternity. Whatever trials you're facing, bring them to God and ask for more of His joy to carry you through them.

READING: Nehemiah 8:1–12

KEY VERSE v10

'Don't be dejected and sad, for the joy of the LORD is your strength!'

If anyone ever needed strength, it's Nehemiah. Nehemiah and his people undertook a huge task in rebuilding the walls of Jerusalem and, as if this wasn't enough, his enemies caused all sorts of trouble to try to stop the building work. Nehemiah must have been sorely tempted more than once to give up, but he still found the strength to carry on. Finally, when the walls were complete, we get an insight into where Nehemiah and all the people were getting their strength from.

In a small way, I can identify with Nehemiah. I remember a social action project my church once organised in our town. Towards the end of a long week, a group of us were digging people's gardens. One woman accepted our help and showed us the state her garden was in. It was a nightmare. There were chest-high weeds and nettles as far as we could see. Two

WEEKEND 28/29 JUL

CONTINUED »

dead rose bushes needed to be uprooted and thrown away. And all of this was covered in rubbish. We were already shattered and clearing up this mess was going to take forever.

We took a deep breath and made a start. Then someone started singing. Soon we were all singing. The afternoon passed in a blur as we dug, cut, sang and told jokes. Before we knew it, the whole garden was clear. What I realised at that moment was what Nehemiah knew thousands of years ago: the joy of the Lord is our strength. When we feel that we can't carry on, God's joy gives us strength and helps us to continue. Nehemiah and his people faced all kinds of trials and came through because God strengthened them. My friends and I faced our own small trial and found that God carried us through that. He can do the same for you.

PRAY

Are you facing a trial today? Don't try to handle it on your own. Ask God to give you more of His joy to strengthen you.

READING: Psalm 42:1–11

KEY VERSE v11

'Why am I discouraged? Why is my heart so sad? I will put my hope in God! I will praise ... my Savior and my God!'

I can't stand Monday mornings. Perhaps you know what I mean. I can't think of a less joyful time of the week. The weekend is over, and I have to get out of bed far too early and take on another week of work. It's even worse if it happens to be raining. Of course, I know I've still got plenty to be thankful about really, but I certainly don't *feel* like praising God on Monday morning. Life is full of Monday mornings, though. Any day can feel like a Monday morning, if you're tired, dealing with a few problems and feeling generally short of joy.

It takes determination to praise God and be joyful on Monday mornings, but that's exactly what the writer of this psalm does. He resolves to praise God despite his problems and, by his example, he challenges us to do the same. Even when we don't *feel* like praising God, we should still *choose* to do that. God is still good, even on Monday mornings. Even if we're not happy, we still have a lot to thank Him and praise Him for. So, whatever's going on, we should still praise Him. We can't always have fun, but we can always have God's joy.

MON 30 JUL

CHALLENGE

The next time you get the 'Monday morning' feeling, choose to praise God anyway.

READING: John 7:37–44

'Anyone who believes in me may come and drink! ... "Rivers of living water will flow from his heart."'

KEY VERSE v38

TUES 31 JUL

My son loves playing with our garden sprinkler. On a hot day, it's a lot of fun to set up the sprinkler in the middle of the lawn, turn it on, then run across the middle of the garden, trying to avoid the spray. It's impossible, obviously. There's so much water around, covering such a wide area, that it just isn't possible to avoid it. Then again, when it's that hot, we don't really want to avoid the water anyway.

Jesus' words remind me of the image of our garden sprinkler. Jesus will put so much life, so much joy into someone who knows Him that it just can't be contained and will burst out of them. Anyone who meets that person will then be drenched in Jesus' life. You must know people who seem to have a knack of spreading joy wherever they go. We can be like this too, if we know Jesus and keep receiving His joy. This doesn't mean that we need to be over-the-top smiley and happy all the time, if that's not the kind of people we are. If we have Jesus' joy in us, it will naturally affect the people around us.

PRAY

Ask Jesus to give you rivers of living water which will refresh the people around you. See how this 'living water' affects the people you meet.

READING: Ecclesiastes 3:1–8

KEY VERSE v4

'A time to cry and a time to laugh.
A time to grieve and a time to dance.'

A couple of months ago, a woman in my church died suddenly. It was a real shock to the whole church and very sad, because she was a real woman of God and everyone loved her. We committed her into God's hands and we knew that she'd gone to a far better place, but it was still difficult for us to come to terms with her death. At times like these, it's right and healthy to grieve.

Soon afterwards, the church had a completely different experience. Another woman was ordained as a priest and we had a huge celebration. This was brilliant, not just for the lady who'd been ordained, but for the church as a whole. Definitely a time to be joyful and have fun!

We all experience joy and grief at different times. Normally it's obvious how we should react in a given situation. We don't need to ask how to react when someone dies, for example. At other times, we may need a little more wisdom and sensitivity about how to behave. We need to be aware of how the people around us might be feeling. But the most important thing to remember is that whatever season of life we're in, whether we're laughing or grieving, God is always with us and always in control.

WED 1 AUG

THINK

What season of life are you in at the moment? Is it right for you to be laughing, grieving or something in between? How does it feel to know that God is with you right now?

READING: 2 Chronicles 7:11–16

'... if my people who are called by my name will humble themselves and pray ... I will hear from heaven ...'

KEY VERSE v14

THURS 2 AUG

CHALLENGE

Set aside a specific time every week to pray with your friends. Make this a regular commitment. Why not set up a prayer room at your church and get your whole youth group praying? Check out www.24-7prayer.com for inspiration.

Someone once told me that our culture teaches us to feast and play, when what we should really be doing is fasting and praying. There's nothing wrong with having fun, but there comes a time when we need to drop the fun stuff and spend time praying instead. In these verses from 2 Chronicles, God promises that when we pray amazing things happen. If we're committed to praying, seeking God and turning away from sin, God does act to forgive us and heal our nation. We can see this in history, too. Every time we have seen God do great and supernatural things, it has started with people being committed to praying. The revivals in the Hebrides in 1949, Los Angeles in 1906, Wales in 1904 and even the birth of Methodism in the 18th century all began with people spending time in intense prayer.

And quite apart from anything extraordinary God might do, just spending time with Him is so valuable. Even if God doesn't seem to change much else through these times, He changes us. God does want us to enjoy life, but He also wants us to spend time with Him. So how can you make time to pray, both on your own and with friends?

READING: Revelation 19:1–10

KEY VERSE v7

'Let us be glad and rejoice, and let us give honor to him. For the time has come for the wedding feast of the Lamb …'

This week, some of my colleagues and I were feeling frustrated about the sheer number of forms we have to fill in at work. Someone piped up: 'I hope there aren't any forms to complete in heaven.' This started us joking about heaven being like the Post Office; having to stand in line, go to the right window when you're called and fill in the right forms in the right way to get in.

Fortunately for all of us, heaven isn't like the Post Office and there won't be any forms to fill in! Heaven isn't even going to be a never-ending church service, with an eternity of hymn singing. (Although I'm sure we'll have plenty to sing about when we see God face to face.) Revelation describes heaven as being a feast – a massive party! Our destiny is an eternal celebration, feasting and enjoying being in God's presence forever – the biggest, longest, best party ever. If life seems tough now, keeping this destiny in mind can encourage us. In the meantime, whenever we have fun, we catch just a little glimpse of what eternity will be like.

FRI 3 AUG

THINK

Take some time out now to have a little fun. Remember that your destiny is a heavenly celebration. Imagine what this might be like.

DISCIPLINE
THE IMPORTANCE OF DISCIPLINE

WEEKEND 4/5 AUG

THINK OF A SMALL child being taught to cross the road safely by an adult. No doubt we all had this kind of instruction when we were younger. But why? What is the purpose of teaching a child to cross the road with care? Surely it is to ensure that they stay safe and that, in time, they will be able to cross the road independently without fear of getting hurt.

Discipline s about being taught to be wiser and more responsible. Most people, when they discipline us, do it for our own good (or at least that is their hope). They do it because they care about us and want the best for us. That doesn't stop us, however, from sometimes finding

READING: Proverbs 19:16–21

> 'Discipline your children while there is hope. Otherwise you will ruin their lives.'

KEY VERSE V18

WEEKEND 4/5 AUG

discipline hard to take. We like to think that we are pretty intelligent people who can do a good job looking out for ourselves. But those who love and care for us have a duty to look out for us, and to discipline us where necessary.

A blunt pencil is made sharper and regains its usefulness only by having bits shaved off. A rose bush can only continue to grow healthily and more beautifully when it is pruned. Sometimes, the process of being disciplined can be painful, and seems almost damaging. But it helps if we view this discipline differently: someone who cares about us is helping us to become the person we ultimately should be.

PRAY

Father God, please help me to respond positively to discipline and to see it as a way of growing. Help me to accept discipline graciously and willingly from those who love and care for me. Amen.

READING: John 8:21–32

'Jesus said to the people who believed in him, "You are truly my disciples if you remain faithful to my teachings."'

KEY VERSE v31

Have you noticed that the word 'discipline' is very similar to the word 'disciple'? Apparently, our word 'disciple' comes from the Latin for 'learner' and the word 'discipline' means 'instruction' or 'teaching'. To be a follower of Jesus is to follow and learn from His teachings. Or, to put it another way, to be a disciple of Jesus is to be subject to His discipline.

When we think of it in this way, discipline is not such a negative concept. Rather, it is something we should strive for. If we want to be genuine followers of Jesus, then we need to follow His teachings and instructions. We need to experience His discipline.

Today's Bible reading highlights that by being His disciples, we can enjoy freedom as a result of knowing the truth (v.32). We often think of discipline as something that limits us, stopping us from doing the things we would like to do. Over the next couple of weeks, we'll explore the idea that discipline actually helps us to be free.

THINK

In what ways do you think discipline might enable us to be more free? How might God discipline us?

READING: Proverbs 3:11–20

KEY VERSE v12

'For the LORD corrects those he loves, just as a father corrects a child in whom he delights.'

A couple of days ago we mentioned that parents usually discipline their children because they love them and want the best for them. We often talk of God as Father and, therefore, it's inevitable that God should have a role in disciplining us. Yet, for many of us, if we stop and think of God disciplining us, it can be hard to pinpoint what that actually involves. Does God punish us by striking us down with a dreadful illness or making it rain all day when we want it to be sunny? In reality, I suspect that this is not usually the case. However, the Bible assures us that God does indeed discipline us. Indeed, today's reading points out that this is because He loves us and we should not be unhappy about receiving His discipline.

Over the next few days we'll be thinking a bit more about what it means to be disciplined by God and what that discipline could look like.

PRAY

Thank You, Father, that You love us as Your children and want the best for us. Help us to accept Your discipline, as its purpose is for us to become better followers of You. Amen.

READING: 2 Samuel 12:1–12

'Because of what you have done, I will cause your own household to rebel against you.'

 **KEY VERSE v11**

WED 8 AUG

Let me give you a bit of background, in case you're not familiar with the story. King David had fallen for a woman who was already married. David slept with her, despite being well aware that this was wrong, and she became pregnant. In the end, David resorted to having her husband murdered, so that he could marry the woman and avoid a scandal.

In Nathan's story, which we read today, David is confronted with what he did. Notice how he reacts with the anger towards the character representing him. We need to face up to the truth when we do wrong. We need to admit what we have done and repent of it.

Although we can be forgiven by God when we sin, as Nathan tells David he has been, this does not free us from the negative consequences of what we've done. This is why learning to obey God and choosing well is so important.

How many times have you prayed something like this: 'God, I'm sorry. Please let everything go back to normal'? If God answered this prayer in the way I would like every time I prayed it, I do not believe that I would fully learn from my mistakes. It is only by facing up to the consequences, knowing that God loves and forgives us, that we are able to move on.

PRAY

Thank You, Father God, that You forgive us when we come to You in repentance. Help us to learn from the consequences of our mistakes. Amen.

READING: Matthew 18:21–35

KEY VERSE v35

'That's what my heavenly Father will do to you if you refuse to forgive your brothers and sisters from your heart.'

Have you ever known a parent for whom it seems that their children can do no wrong? Even if their children act in a nasty, rude and cruel way, to their parents they are still little angels, perfect in every way. This is a good example of exactly why we need to have our mistakes pointed out to us and why we need to be disciplined.

Today's reading describes a man who behaved in a particularly nasty way. Despite the kindness shown to him in regard to his own debt, he refused to have mercy on someone who was in debt to him. The consequences were that he was punished by being thrown into prison.

If we fail to show mercy and forgiveness towards others then we end up in a mess of anger and bitterness. God isn't cruel and doesn't 'torture' us Himself, but maybe He sometimes leaves us to the consequences of our actions: to teach us and make us more loving and forgiving. God is faithful to us, even though sometimes we are not faithful to Him. Whatever we have done wrong, He is prepared to forgive. If we have been given this grace, then we also have a responsibility to show the same grace to others. If we do not, expect to be taught a lesson!

THURS 9 AUG

CHALLENGE

Who was the last person who hurt you? Have you forgiven this person? Is there anyone you're holding a grudge against? Think about the love and forgiveness Jesus has shown you and make an effort to show the same love and forgiveness to other people.

READING: 1 Peter 1:3–9

'...trials will show that your faith is genuine. It is being tested as fire tests and purifies gold...'

KEY VERSE v7

FRI 10 AUG

One way in which we can receive discipline and be made more into the people God wants us to be is by being allowed to go through difficult times. You may remember that last weekend we talked about the need for pencils to be sharpened and rose bushes to be pruned. If you were trying to purify a metal, such as gold, you would subject it to high temperatures. This would help you to refine it and to separate the impurities from the molten gold.

Today's verses tell us that our faith can be refined by going through trials. Even Jesus faced difficult times, for example when being tempted by the devil in the desert (Mark 1:12–13; Luke 4:1–13). But the Bible assures us that when we go through difficult times and times of temptation, God will give us the strength to get through them (1 Cor. 10:13). Difficult times force us to stay close to God, relying on Him rather than on ourselves. They help us to learn more about Him, and we come out of the refining fire stronger and more mature than we were before.

THINK

How do you feel when you are going through a difficult time? Can you look back at times in your life that have been hard and see how God has strengthened you and brought you closer to Him through them?

READING: Proverbs 5:1-14

KEY VERSE v12

'You will say, "How I hated discipline! If only I had not ignored all the warnings!"'

How do you feel if you are told off in public? I can vividly remember a Victorian day at school as a child. I needed to leave part-way through the school day to attend a medical appointment. My father had arranged with the teacher that he would come in, dressed as a Victorian headmaster, to collect me. I knew nothing of this arrangement. Later on during the day, my dad entered the room in his robes and proceeded to shout at me, insisting that I go with him to the headmaster's office. I was devastated. Not only had I been told off in front of all my classmates, but I hadn't even been doing anything wrong in the first place!

Not many of us like being disciplined, and we may be tempted to ignore those who try to set us straight. But

WEEKEND 11/12 AUG

try to imagine what might happen if we do not have our mistakes pointed out and made clear to us. Watching someone make bad decisions can be like watching a horrific crash in slow motion.

Today's reading highlights that those people who choose to ignore wise instruction usually live to regret it. As a child, my cousin was allowed to drink her juice from a wine glass at a special occasion. She insisted on holding the glass at the bottom of the stem, despite protests from her mother who told her that the glass would break. Sure enough, the glass did break and she was made to look silly for not following her mother's advice. If we don't pay attention to those who try to instruct us and discipline us, we run the risk of embarrassment or even public disgrace.

CHALLENGE

How do you respond to discipline? What might be the consequences if you choose to ignore those who try to help you by disciplining you?

READING: Proverbs 5:21–23

KEY VERSE v22

'An evil man is held captive by his own sins; they are ropes that catch and hold him.'

We might long to be free from rules that restrict us from doing what we want to do. Many people like to tell us that rules are there to be broken. But can you imagine a school without rules or a society with no laws?

Imagine that you and a group of your friends sailed off to a desert island and established a new community. Very quickly you would need to develop a set of rules in order to prevent chaos from reigning. What sort of laws might these be? Why are they so important?

In actual fact, being free from rules or laws does not lead to freedom, but chaos. If we are allowed to do what we want, then today's reading tells us that we become trapped and caught by our own wrongdoing. Rules protect us and help us to live our lives fully. Because we have laws and a police force to enforce those laws, we can go about our daily lives feeling secure. We are set free by the laws we have in place.

THINK

Think of those places where people do live in fear: perhaps a country with a corrupt police force or no clear/fair government in power. Pray that God would help to bring about a stable and fair government and set these people free.

READING: Romans 6:12–23

'But now you are free from the power of sin and have become slaves of God.'

KEY VERSE v22

TUES 14 AUG

If someone is in authority over you, does it mean that you have to do everything they tell you to do? In most circumstances, probably not. We have free will and, as such, can decide whether or not to do what a parent, teacher or other person in authority asks us to do. However, we will face the consequences of any decision we take.

When I was a child, my father and I made a request on a radio show for a message to be read out and a song to be played for my mum and my brother. We did not want to tell them what we had done, but asked them to listen to the radio show. My mother duly did so, but my brother refused to listen, choosing instead to watch something on the television. As a consequence, he missed hearing the request and his name mentioned on the radio.

Sometimes, when we are too stubborn to do what someone who loves us asks us to do we miss out on a possible good consequence. Today's Bible reading tells us that the reward for obeying God is eternal life. This is in contrast to the pain that results from being a slave to sin.

CHALLENGE

Is God calling you to do something in particular, or to give something up? Are you resisting Him in this? Take a brave step today and decide to obey Him. It might be scary, but it'll definitely be worth it.

READING: Hebrews 12:1–13

KEY VERSE v10

'But God's discipline is always good for us, so that we might share in his holiness.'

In order to achieve anything in life, we often have to endure hardship along the way. For academic success, we need to study hard. To achieve sporting success, we need to be disciplined in our training.

Today's passage reminds us that the Christian life is not always easy. Sometimes we might even feel like giving up. Marathon runners talk about 'hitting the wall' when they feel as if they can go no further. However, when they keep on pushing past this wall of exhaustion, they are somehow able to go on. Today's passage tells us that when we feel like this, we should fix our eyes on Jesus and allow ourselves to be inspired by Him.

God isn't going to simply remove all the obstacles from our path and make our lives easy. We don't become Christians in order to have an easier life. However, when we are struggling, we should be assured that God is there with us as our coach. Unlike an earthly coach or father, God really does always know best. We really can trust in Him and His instructions for our life.

WED 15 AUG

CHALLENGE

Today's reading talks about throwing off the things that hold us back such as sin. Is there anything that you think God, your master coach, is calling you to throw off? Accept His discipline and instruction because He truly does know what is best for you.

READING: Romans 8:28-39

> '... nothing in all creation will ever be able to separate us from the love of God ...'

KEY VERSE v39

THURS 16 AUG

In Romans 8 Paul challenges us to see the big picture. As we reflected yesterday, during times of trouble it is so easy to think that God has abandoned us, and yet the Bible and history is full of stories that show how wrong that idea is.

Paul is clear that God doesn't always seem to help, but that 'God causes everything to work together'. So a situation might not be what we had hoped for or expected, but God is still very much in control. He causes things to happen so that we become more like Jesus, and we will see this process of sanctification (becoming holy, more like God) complete when we are glorified, in heaven. The passage then goes on to highlight that suffering is not the end of the story, but is just a part of the story. God cares so much for us that He gave up Jesus. But through Jesus' suffering God was able to work for good.

When we are in the midst of a time of discipline or trial, we need to remember that God holds the bigger picture. He knows what He is doing. Are we prepared to put our trust in Him?

PRAY

Father God, help us in the midst of trouble, pain and suffering to see Your big picture; and to understand that victory is Yours and that nothing in all creation will ever be able to separate us from Your love. Amen.

READING: 2 Thessalonians 3:6–13

KEY VERSE v9

'We did this … in order to offer ourselves as a model for you to imitate.' (NIV)

For much of the last fortnight, we have looked at our response to being disciplined ourselves. But this is only one side of the story. As we get older, we are increasingly faced with taking on the role of disciplining others and setting an example to younger people. Perhaps you help out with children's work at church, mentor a younger pupil at school or earn money through babysitting; or maybe you have younger brothers or sisters. Even if you can't think of a specific situation that is like one of the situations listed above, I have no doubt that some younger people, somewhere, look up to you in some way.

Today's reading gives some wise principles for all those of us involved in disciplining and setting an example to others. Are we doing it for the satisfaction of feeling powerful and exploiting people? Or are we exercising our authority in a godly way? Our motivation in leading and disciplining people should be to serve them, help them and give them a model of godly living for them to copy.

FRI 17 AUG

THINK

Think about the people who look up to you. How do you teach them, instruct them and help set them free to live wise and godly lives? After all, that's what the ultimate aim of discipling and discipline should be.

JESUS

WEEKEND 18/19 AUG

FULLY MAN + FULLY GOD

IT MIGHT BE August, but there's a distinctly Christmassy feel to this final part of 'Jesus, fully man and fully God'. We'll be looking at Old Testament prophecies concerning Jesus' life and ministry, many of which are often read at Christmas. But strip away the tinsel and the warm, fuzzy Christmas feeling from these prophecies, and we're left with some very powerful and very inspiring truths about who Jesus is.

There are approximately 300 Old Testament prophecies about Jesus, and George Heron, a French mathematician, calculated that the odds of one man fulfilling even 40 of them are 1 in 10

READING: Isaiah 9:6–7

> 'For a child is born to us, a son is given to us. The government will rest on his shoulders.'

KEY VERSE V6

to the power of 157. That is a 1 followed by 157 zeros! In other words, it's no accident that Jesus fulfils all of these prophecies. From the beginning, it was God's plan to send Jesus into the world and, even hundreds of years before Jesus was born, God spoke through the prophets about exactly who Jesus was and what He would do. When Jesus came, He fulfilled God's plans for Him.

The wonderful prophecy from Isaiah 9 helps us to understand the type of kingdom Jesus came to build: one which will rest on His shoulders, where He will reign as a Wonderful Counsellor, a Mighty God, an Everlasting Father and a Prince of Peace. This kingdom will never end. It doesn't really sound like any of our unstable earthly kingdoms, governments or states, does it?

And how will this kingdom come into being? Through war? Through revolution? Through a media campaign? No! It's already started – through a baby born to us; through a Saviour who came into the world as one of us.

THINK

Jesus came as a tiny baby, but also as a King; mighty, but also peaceful and bringing justice. What do these truths tell us about His kingdom?

READING: Micah 5:2-4

'But you, O Bethlehem Ephrathah, are only a small village among all the people of Judah.'

KEY VERSE v2

MON 20 AUG

Are you good at reading instructions? Do you always read all the questions on an examination paper before starting? Do you fill in a form, then realise that it should have been completed in black ink? Are instructions a bore? Would you rather get on and play the computer game than learn about the different levels?

I love the way the Bible is so detailed in its prophecies concerning Jesus and His birth – even down to its location in Bethlehem. This passage from Micah (a contemporary of Isaiah, living 700 years before Jesus' birth) is preparing those who read the instructions, telling them that Jesus is coming.

This village of Bethlehem was home to Naomi, Ruth and Boaz. It was the home of Jesse and the shepherd boy, David (who later killed Goliath and became king). Although small, Bethlehem was a very important village.

Micah tells us that from David's town will come a King whose *'origins are from the distant past'*. The baby Jesus in the manger is the same Jesus who was present at the creation of the world; the distant past! This human baby's origins are from beyond time and space! Awesome!

THINK

The Creator God of Genesis, whom heaven and earth cannot contain, is present in this tiny baby in a manger! God condensed – somehow in some amazing, unexplainable way – into the form of a child!

READING: Isaiah 7:10–15

KEY VERSE v14

'All right then, the Lord himself will give you the sign. Look! The virgin will conceive a child.'

Can you imagine the embarrassment – I'm standing under a street sign that reads 'Rothschild Place' and, with a confused look on my face, I stop a passing stranger to ask: 'Excuse me, could you tell me where Rothschild Place is?' The man, a tourist from Serbia, smiled and pointed upwards! It was so obvious! It was right under (or even above) my stupid nose!

Here we see a huge sign from God telling the whole world that Jesus will be different from any human ever born. He'll be born of a virgin. There's lots of controversy concerning this verse. Some theologians believe that this verse simply means that Mary was a 'young girl' and not a virgin. However, Mary was approximately 14 years old, from a very religious family, and engaged to Joseph. Unlike in today's society, 2,000 years ago this would have meant that she was definitely a virgin.

Isaiah's prophecy – roughly 700 years before Jesus' birth – set the Messiah apart from any other human being who has ever walked on planet Earth. We are all a result of two human parents. To fulfil the words of this prophecy, Jesus was born of a human mother but a heavenly Father: fully man yet fully God!

TUES 21 AUG

CHALLENGE

Do you really believe that Jesus was born of a virgin? How does this belief change your view of Jesus?

READINGS: Isaiah 7:13–15; Luke 1:26–38

'The virgin ... will give birth to a son and will call him Immanuel (which means "God is with us").'

KEY VERSE: Isa. 7:14

WED 22 AUG

Read Luke's account and imagine that you're a 14-year-old girl from a small town in Galilee, promised in marriage to a carpenter. You discover that you're pregnant, yet you've never had sex. What do you do? Rumours would spread like wildfire! So why did God choose to come to earth in this highly awkward way?

Have you ever wondered why God chose to visit earth as a tiny baby? Why didn't He write a message in the sky? The reason He chose to come as a tiny baby, born to a teenager in a stable, lies in this word *Immanuel* (God with us). Jesus shared our human feelings: hunger, sorrow, pain, loneliness – and even the experience of being born.

As we've studied so far this week, Jesus is God 'with skin on' (incarnate), sent to communicate with us (the Word) and He resembles God completely (the Son of God). We learn today that He dwelt with us on earth, experiencing our human emotions (Immanuel).

CHALLENGE

If Jesus truly understands being human, then He will completely understand how you feel today: when you are tired, lonely, angry or depressed. Take your feelings to Jesus and ask our Immanuel to help you.

READING: Isaiah 50:5–9

KEY VERSE v6

'I offered my back to those who beat me and my cheeks to those who pulled out my beard.'

THURS 23 AUG

This might feel like a bit of a sudden change of direction. We've spent the past few days looking in detail at Jesus' birth and now suddenly we're talking about His death. But while we're thinking about Jesus being born, it's so important for us to remember the *reason* Jesus came to earth. As important as His birth and ministry were, the most important aspect of Jesus' life was His death on the cross. Without this sacrificial death for each one of us, we would have no access to the God of heaven.

Babies are wonderful, but the really exciting, fascinating part is watching them grow up and seeing the people they become. Even when Jesus was a baby, God's plan was for Him to become a man; a perfect man who would be crucified, take the punishment we deserved and deal with our sin. Even in His birth, Jesus was born to die on the cross for us! It's wonderful to remember Jesus the baby, but if we don't remember Jesus the man, we're missing something really important and utterly amazing.

PRAY

Thank You, Lord, for coming into the world as a baby. Thank You for following Your Father's plan perfectly. Help me to remember that the reason You came to earth as a baby was to die on the cross.

READING: Luke 2:1–20

> 'The Savior – yes, the Messiah, the Lord – has been born today in Bethlehem, the city of David!'

KEY VERSE v11

FRI 24 AUG

It's how you end a game that counts! Many football teams can play really well for 70 minutes, but then seem to run out of steam – allowing the opposition time and space to finish them off. They start off with lots of energy but finish poorly.

A lot of people focus on Christ's arrival as a baby into this world: how He was born in a stable, wrapped in strips of cloth and laid in a manger; how shepherds, and later kings, visited, and countless angels sang on the hillside. However, it wasn't Jesus' beginning that counts for us as sinners, but it was His end: His sacrificial death on the cross, enabling us to receive forgiveness for our sins and eternal life with God.

If Jesus had simply been born miraculously and then, aged 33, stepped off our planet and gone back to heaven, we would have no access to the throne room of God. If Jesus had healed thousands of sick people then teleported back to HQ, we would have no forgiveness of sins. Let's remember how Jesus ended His time on earth, not just how He began it. Let's take time to thank Jesus for His birth, His life and, especially, His death on the cross.

THINK

Every year of your life you may have heard the story of Jesus' Nativity. Think about this: none of this story would be worth celebrating had Jesus not gone to the cross to take our punishment for us and to give us eternal life.

READING: Daniel 7:13–18

KEY VERSE v13 — 'As my vision continued that night, I saw someone like a son of man coming with the clouds of heaven.'

I had a friend at school who was very shy and quiet. I don't think any of us expected him to sign up for the school play. When the performance came, we watched open-mouthed as this guy was transformed before our eyes. He just seemed to come to life on the stage. Of course, he'd always had this side to him, we'd just never seen it before.

When you see someone you know in a completely different context, you can sometimes see an entirely new side to them. We've already seen a very human Jesus; Jesus as a tiny baby and as a man suffering and dying for us. But we now shift our attention, and focus on Jesus in a different context, the context of heaven. As we do that, we see a very different side of Jesus.

WEEKEND 25/26 AUG

CONTINUED ▶

We see the divine Jesus; the transcendent Jesus. In this passage from Daniel we see Jesus referred to as the 'son of man'. This phrase is one which Jesus used Himself a number of times in the Gospels to explain that He is God in human form.

Here we see a very different Jesus from the baby in the stable and the carpenter in His workshop. Here we see Jesus in the clouds (Rev. 1:7), coming before the 'Ancient One', who is God the Father. Jesus stands before the eternal Creator of the universe and is led into His presence after completing His mission on earth. Jesus is now seated with the Father in heaven and represents us (yes, little us!) before the Mighty Father (Heb. 7:24–25). This image of the 'son of man' defines our Jesus: fully human, yet fully God; the Messiah, the Christ, our God in the flesh!

PRAY

Thank You, Jesus, that You represent humankind in heaven. Thank You that You're seated at God's right hand: our Saviour, our God-man.

READING: Psalm 22:1–31

KEY VERSE v1

'My God, my God, why have you abandoned me? Why are you so far away when I groan for help?'

The psalmist, David, wrote this famous prophecy about the Messiah (Jesus) roughly 1,000 years before Jesus' death on a cross, and hundreds of years before crucifixion was even invented! These words show the huge cost of Jesus' separation from His Father. At that point, Jesus became sin, our sin: God the Father (who is totally pure and holy) and His Son were separated by sin as Jesus took our punishment for us. It's almost impossible to imagine the pain and despair Jesus would have felt as He was temporarily completely abandoned by His Father.

It wasn't the cruel nails that held Jesus to the cross: it was His unending love for us. As the sky grew dark and the thunder rumbled, the curtain in the Temple (that for centuries had symbolically separated man from God) was torn from top to bottom. There's no longer anything to separate us from God. We're free to know God and to have a relationship with Him, if we only ask for it. This relationship with God cost Jesus everything He had, but it's now free for us.

MON 27 AUG

THINK

Have you ever really counted the cost Jesus paid for you on the cross: the physical, emotional and spiritual separation from His Father; the sin of the whole world on His body?

READING: Hebrews 1:1–3

KEY VERSE v3

'The Son radiates God's own glory and expresses the very character of God ...'

TUES 28 AUG

I was walking through London a while ago when a policeman stopped me by the kerbside and asked me to: 'Wait here please, Sir!' I was confused at first, but then I saw a royal entourage pass by within feet of me and I caught a glimpse of Prince Charles through the dark windows of his stretch limo. I was within three feet of the future King of England. This made me excited, yet also a little nervous – to be so close to someone so famous.

In many ways, Prince Charles represents the Queen, but Jesus does far more than simply represent God. Here, in the book of Hebrews, we are told that Jesus *radiates God's own glory*. He expresses *the very character of God* in the way He conducts Himself and in the way He lived life on earth. Jesus is more than an ambassador, more than a Prince of heaven: He is more than a likeness to His Father; He is a window through which the nature and character of God radiate.

Do the love and character of God shine out through your life? People should look at you and say: 'There really is something different about him/her.'

CHALLENGE

Jesus is the radiance of the Father's glory. If you want to see what God looks like, then look at Jesus and re-examine how He lived, how He spoke and how He treated all types of people. Should you change something about the way you live to reflect Him better?

READING: Colossians 1:15–23

KEY VERSE v17

'He existed before anything else, and he holds all creation together.'

Jesus expresses the very character of God. This means Jesus has God's power to create and sustain. Being completely God, Jesus was involved in creation and He also holds the whole universe together. Jesus is, quite simply, the most important Being in creation. Without Him, everything would fall apart.

A friend of mine was once part of a crew for a long-distance yacht race. In the middle of a rough sea, the crew had to take down the mast and my friend was handed a metal pin which normally held the mast up. Without this pin, it would be impossible to put the mast back up and the yacht would cease to function. Predictably, my friend promptly dropped the pin, causing total panic! Jesus is essential. Whether or not we choose to notice Him, He makes the whole of creation function.

Of course, if Jesus holds everything together, that includes us. Our bodies, our minds and our emotions are gifts from Jesus and they only function by His grace. Jesus deserves to be 'before anything else', the single most important Person in our lives. This is a challenge because, let's face it, we're all tempted to rely on other things to keep us going: money, looking good, status, our friends, or even drink and drugs.

WED 29 AUG

THINK

Is Jesus 'before anything else' in your life? Are you relying on Him to hold you together? Or are you depending on something else? Pray about it.

READING: 2 Corinthians 5:19–21

'So we are Christ's ambassadors ... We speak for Christ when we plead, "Come back to God!"'

KEY VERSE v20

THURS 30 AUG

As recently as 2008 the state of Kosovo became an independent country. Formerly part of the Serbian nation, and for many years under the rule of the Iron Curtain superstate of Yugoslavia, Kosovo became a nation in its own right. One of the first things to happen in a newly-recognised state is the setting up of embassies in the capital city by foreign ambassadors. The ambassadors represent their own countries and through their embassies come aid, commerce, education, health care and links with the outside world.

In 2 Corinthians we're told that we are Christ's ambassadors. The Church is God's embassy and God appeals through us to the whole world to come back to Him. Notice that we don't make the appeal for ourselves – it is God who makes *His* appeal *through* us. We are merely His mouthpiece, His ambassadors, His representatives on earth.

Whenever you struggle to find the right words while trying to talk to your friends about Jesus, remember that you are God's ambassador. If you're willing, He will speak through you and use you to communicate to others.

PRAY

Jesus, please help me when I speak to my friends about You. Speak through me and make me Your ambassador. Lord, I am willing to be used by You to speak to the world.

READING: Matthew 28:18–20

KEY VERSE v19

'Therefore, go and make disciples of all the nations, baptizing them in the name of the Father and the Son and the Holy Spirit.'

So what have you gained from our series on 'Jesus, fully man and fully God'? Perhaps you've got a new perspective on Jesus as a person who experienced every kind of human need and emotion, just as we do. Or maybe you've been struck by the heavenly, transcendent Jesus, who is fully God and absolutely awesome. Whatever you've learned, I hope you've been inspired to know Jesus a little better today than you did yesterday, and a little better tomorrow than you do today. I also hope you've been inspired to tell other people about this amazing God we follow.

Matthew's closing lines document Jesus' words: our mission is to go and tell all the nations the good news of Jesus Christ, making them followers of Him. Then they can make the decision to be baptised publicly into the power and authority of the Father, Son and Holy Spirit – taking up Christ's mission for themselves! As we saw yesterday, we are Jesus' ambassadors. A crucial part of this is telling people about Him.

Why not commit to telling one person a day about Jesus? Hope Revolution have some great ideas as to how you could go about this. Visit www.hope-revolution.com to find out more.

FRI 31 AUG

PRAY

Lord Jesus, thank You for being awesome and thank You for making me Your ambassador. Please help me to speak up for You.

METTLE MAY–AUGUST 2012

ORDER FORM

4 EASY WAYS TO ORDER:

1. For credit/debit card payment, call 01252 784710 (Mon–Fri, 9.30am – 5pm)
2. Visit our Online Store at www.cwr.org.uk/store
3. Send this form together with a cheque made payable to CWR to: CWR, Waverley Abbey House, Waverley Lane, Farnham, Surrey GU9 8EP
4. Visit a Christian bookshop

YOUR DETAILS

Name:

CWR ID No. (if known):

Address:

Postcode:

Telephone No. (for queries):

Email:

SUBSCRIPTIONS° (NON DIRECT DEBIT)	QTY	PRICE (INCLUDING P&P)			TOTAL
		UK	Europe	Elsewhere	
Mettle (1yr, 3 issues)		£13.80	£15.90	£18.00*	
(Subscription prices already include postage and packing)				TOTAL **B**	

Please circle which four-month issue you would like your subscription to commence from:

| Jan–Apr | May–Aug | Sep–Dec |

*Order direct from CWR or from your National Distributor. For a list of our National Distributors and contact details, visit www.cwr.org.uk/distributors